SHOW UP:

*Finding Love For
Independent Women*

CHRISTINE CHANG
Copyright © 2020 by Christine Chang

Please visit www.christinechang.com for more information.

ISBN:

978-1-7350970-1-5

Edited by Leigh Ann Zerr

Formatting and Cover Design by Anne Tso

Cover Photo by Sara Stark

For my mom, the woman who
taught me to be independent so that
I could have more options in life.

TABLE OF CONTENTS

Ch. 1   I Finally Found It: How I Met My Kick-ass Husband ... 8

Ch. 2   It's All About Intentions ... 12

Ch. 3   The Time I Was Cheated On ... 14

Ch. 4   Is There Something Wrong With Me? ... 21

Ch. 5   Career Success ≠ Relationship Success ... 24

Ch. 6   You Are Not Alone ... 26

Ch. 7   Why Take My Advice? ... 27

Ch. 8   Are You Stepping Up To Bat? ... 29

Ch. 9   My Worst Nightmare Realized ... 31

Ch. 10   Self-Awareness Is Key ... 33

Ch. 11   What Does Your Best Look Like? ... 35

Ch. 12   The Intimidation Factor ... 37

Ch. 13   Breaking Patterns ... 39

Ch. 14   Are You Open Though? ... 41

Ch. 15   Pay Attention to What You Want ... 44

Ch. 16   It's Not Always Rainbows And Butterflies ... 47

Ch. 17   Timing Matters ... 49

Ch. 18   The Moment I Knew ... 50

Ch. 19   More On Healing ... 51

Ch. 20   The Real You ... 61

Ch. 21   Tapping Into Your Soft Side ... 62

Ch. 22   Take Some Time To Daydream ... 65

Ch. 23   Be Kind To Yourself ... 67

Ch. 24   Lessons From My Dog ... 68

Ch. 25   Resilience................................70

Ch. 26   Be Honest With Who You Are 74

Ch. 27   How To Build Confidence.......................76

Ch. 28   Show Yourself Some Love......................79

Ch. 29   Are You Telling Yourself the Truth?..................81

Ch. 30   Passion And Plateaus............................87

Ch. 31   Name Your Non-Negotiables 89

Ch. 32   The Panther And The Tortoise 91

Ch. 33   Adjust Your Expectations 93

Ch. 34   Finding a Well-Rounded Happiness................94

Ch. 35   Increase Your Happiness 96

Ch. 36   Keep It Real. Keep It Honest.....................97

Ch. 37   When Your Needs Just Don't Align.................100

Ch. 38   Set Your Intention While Dating 103

Ch. 39   Seek Feedback From Those You Trust 104

Ch. 40   Where Are All the Good Men? 106

Ch. 41   Three Reasons It's Easier To Live An Authentic Life...111

Ch. 42   How To Be Your Best Self 113

Ch. 43   Some Final Advice On Dating 116

Ch. 44   How Do You Know You've Found "The One"?........118

– Preface –

One thing I kept wondering when I was single was, "Is there something wrong with me?"

If you are reading this book, a similar question may have popped into your mind.

I'll tell you right now. No, there is nothing wrong with you.

Being an independent, capable woman in today's dating world can be tricky to navigate. We definitely aren't living in a Disney movie! I'm a huge Disney fan by the way, but some of those old stories are really fucked up. Recently I watched the original 1937 Snow White with my 4 year old niece. At the end of the movie, Snow White is literally laying dead in a glass coffin, and then Prince Charming rides up on a white horse to kiss and save her.

It was my niece's first time seeing that film. When I asked her what she wants to be when she grows up, she said, "A princess!"

Crap, what did I just do?

Today, gender roles are changing, and the reasons we get into relationships are changing.

"He's intimidated by you." Have you heard that one before?

As a fellow career woman who's been through the dating struggle before I (finally!) met my husband, the purpose of this book is to help navigate some of the frustrations you may encounter, and what you can do to bring you closer to meeting your perfect match.

In this book I share some of my personal stories ("why can't I just get this relationship thing right?") as well as questions I asked myself to gain more self-awareness through the process. These were crucial points in preparing me to show up to meet my husband.

Throughout the book I give action steps and ask you some of the same questions I asked myself. They are simple questions to help you get clear on what you want and what is truly important to you, so that you can break patterns and be that person who is, "relationship goals!"

Clarity = Confidence

I FINALLY FOUND IT

How I Met My Kick-Ass Husband

People often ask how I met my husband, so we'll start there.

It was a Sunday. I showered and put on a lavender satin blouse. The weather must have been dry because the static from my blouse kept making my hair fly everywhere. I met up with a couple girlfriends to have brunch, and then we went shopping in Venice Beach.

We popped in and out of boutiques all day, for so long that we got hungry again. We stumbled into another restaurant and decided to indulge in desserts and champagne. As the sun was setting (and one thousand extra calories later), we decided to call it a day and head home.

In LA you can usually get an Uber immediately - in five minutes or less. We watched on the map as our driver drove around the neighborhood in circles. Ten minutes went by. Where was he? Was he lost?

As we waited, a man yelled, "Chang!"

My former clients - Julie Benz and Rich Orosco walked around the corner. I had photographed their wedding.

"What are you doing here, Chang?"

"We're waiting for our Uber," I said.

Rich proceeded to introduce me to their three guy friends, who were all ridiculously handsome. I'm talking one played Spartacus on TV (literally), another was an actor who looked like the damn prince in Snow White, and the third was a Danish blue-eyed soccer player with long, wavy, perfectly fallen hair.

"We're going inside for dinner. Why don't you come join us?"

I wanted to but didn't want to seem desperate. I flashed my girlfriends a look.

Luckily females have an intuitive sixth sense and they said, "Why don't you stay? We're gonna go home."

In order to say yes to their invite but also look nonchalant, I told them I have a friend who works at the bar down the street (which, I really did).

"I'm going to see if she's working and say hi to her. If she isn't I'll come in for dinner."

Rich said, "Ok... we'll be on the back patio. Come join if you like."

I called my friend who worked at the bar I was talking about. I prayed she wouldn't answer so I could immediately join them for dinner. (By the way, I'm aware I could have lied and said I tried to call her when really I didn't, but... integrity).

Four rings to voicemail. Yes! Thank you baby Jesus.

I walked through the dim hipster restaurant onto the back patio. Ivy climbed up the brick walls. Servers wore denim shirts. The tables were made of reclaimed wood. I spotted Drake the rapper eating dinner with a buddy, and then Julie and Rich's group in the back corner.

Upon walking up they said, "Heeeey, you made it!"

At that time I noticed there was one more guy at the table I had not met yet - a very handsome (and responsible-looking) salt and pepper man wearing white pants and a grey sweater.

"This is Pete. He's the CFO of the restaurant and he's hosting us tonight."

He was sitting and looked up at me. I looked at him. The feeling was calm. A familiar knowing - like a feeling of home.

He asked if I wanted to take his seat because he was sweating by the blazing heat lamps. I get cold anytime the weather drops below 70, so I said sure. I took his seat and he sat in the booth seat next to me.

As everyone was talking, I saw from my peripherals he was watching me. Throughout dinner he asked me a zillion questions, not really talking to anyone else. I learned he was a soccer fan, but he didn't even give the Danish Fabio soccer player the time of day.

I knew he was interested, and my gut told me he was worth getting to know. Years of my personal growth work kicked in. My intuition was ready and listening.

After the server cleared the table, all the guys wanted to take a group photo. I volunteered to take it. I got out of my chair and backed up, turned the phone sideways, and bent forward to get the perfect shot.

Drake brushed my butt with his elbow and then said sorry because apparently I put my butt within six inches from where he was sitting. It was an accident, I swear.

After dinner we walked out of the restaurant.

"Where did you park, Chang?"

"On Lincoln Blvd. I took an Uber here."

Pete said, "I can give you a ride... I just have to bike back to my place to get my truck. It's right around that block."

Typical, independent, don't-want-to-inconvenience-others me said, "No that's ok. It's easy for me to call an Uber."

My clients shot me a big smile and said, "Let Pete drive you to your car."

Sigh. I said ok.

Pete asked me to jump on the handlebars of his bike. His bike was tall as hell (Pete is 6'4") and I couldn't fully sit on the handlebars because the brake wires were there, but we managed to get to his truck without face planting into the asphalt.

When he pulled over to drop me off he looked at me and said, "So, I'd love to take you out to dinner..."

And that's how I met my husband.

Now let's talk about the years I went through before this moment, because they definitely weren't all sunshine and rainbows!

- 2 -

IT'S ALL ABOUT INTENTIONS
How I Adjusted My Mindset To Be Content With Single Life

I've learned that to live a life you love, you have to be clear on what you want.

I always believed I'd be happier in a relationship.

My first two relationships both lasted several years, and while it was fun in the beginning, the remainder of the time felt "eh," like being tied to an anchor. I did things just to make it work, and I was not happy.

That is crazy if you think about it. **Why would I choose something that doesn't make me happy?**

What I realized was that I was unclear on my intention. My intention was to be in a relationship. I would meet a guy who was nice and think: being in a relationship equals happiness, right?

[long buzzer sound]

What my intention should have been was to be happy and fulfilled. *That* is living the life I want no matter what my external circumstances look like. To be truthful, even though I'm married now and love my husband to pieces, I would still feel fulfilled spending time with friends and family, nurturing my career, and doing hobbies that light me up. I feel whole - with or without a relationship.

How do you know if you're on the right track to fulfillment?

I've experienced that listening to your emotions is the best indicator to knowing if you're on the right track. YOU know when you feel good or when you don't feel good. YOU know when you are thriving or when you feel sad on the inside.

Now I'm much more clear on what the purpose of being in a relationship is for me. Not to have someone around because I'm lonely, because I think I'm supposed to for societal standards, or to boost my self-worth (PSA: anywhere outside of you is a bad place to look for it), but because that person is supportive, empathetic, funny, inspiring, and lights up my life.

So let's get right to it.

ACTION STEP:

Why do you want to be in a relationship?
What does an amazing relationship look
like to you? What would it **feel like**?

THE TIME I WAS CHEATED ON

And How I Learned From It

A few years before I met Pete, my dating life was already challenging and unfulfilling. Then I was cheated on. Talk about icing on the cake.

Being cheated on took a LONG time for me to emotionally recover from. It did, however, spark the greatest personal growth journey of my life so far.

Owen was from Chicago. I met him during a trip to Mexico. He was aggressive in pursuing me, and I quickly fell for him.

A few months into our relationship, I met one of his ex-girlfriends – Kelly. Kelly was awesome and hugged me like a bestie. She had a sparkle in her eye and I was comfortable with her. I loved that my boyfriend could remain on good terms with his ex (as I am with most of mine). She was a confident, warm woman. I could tell their relationship had closure. All good signs, right?

Then another ex came into the picture – Megan. The way he talked about Megan was odd, not to mention he hesitated to introduce me to her. I didn't have a good feeling about it, but decided it was fair to trust him unless he gave me a valid reason not to (though him having hesitation to introduce me was a huge flag in and of itself).

What I learned: ***Never question your intuition.***

Everything changed when I went on a volunteer trip to Africa for two weeks. He picked me up from the airport and something felt off. I had a dream while in Africa that he cheated on me, and I wondered if it was me making things up or if I indeed had the right intuition.

I had never done this before and wanted to keep respect for my partner, but something wasn't sitting right. When he went upstairs to use the bathroom, I grabbed his cell phone from the coffee table and picked it up.

In one short scroll of a text conversation with Megan, I knew EVERYTHING. I put the phone down as he came down the stairs.

Me: "Hey, can I ask you something?"

Owen: "Sure babe."

Me: "When you were in Chicago, you said you were with family the whole time and didn't see any friends."

Owen: "Yeah."

Me: "You didn't see any of your old friends?"

Owen: "Well I saw Megan, but only because I had to get some of my old stuff back."

Me: "You never told me that."

Owen: "I didn't think it was notable."

I look down at his watch.

Me: "Where'd you get that watch from?"

Owen: "Oh my mom gave it to me."

(In the texts he had said to her, "Thank you so much for the watch.")

I'm sitting there now livid, perplexed at how he was ok with straight up lying to my face.

Me: "... Ok. Have you ever done anything with Megan that would be considered inappropriate since we've been together?"

Owen: Hugs me (no hesitation whatsoever), "Oh my god baaabe, noooo. I would NEVER do that."

I pulled back and stared at him. It was a raised eyebrow look-of-death stare that communicated, "You lying piece of shit."

His shoulders cowered ever so slightly.

I paused for a few seconds thinking about how to move forward. I decided to be calm and logical about it.

Me: "Ok. I have to apologize for doing this, but while you were upstairs I looked through your phone. I did it because I haven't had a good feeling about you and Megan for the last month. So I'm going to ask you again. Have you done anything inappropriate with her since we've been together?"

At this point he looked at the ground. I felt like a mom scolding her kid and I won't lie, a sick part of me found great pleasure in catching him.

He didn't say anything for a long time. I watched him as he stared at the floor. Five minutes of complete silence went by.

Then he said, "I don't know what to say. I feel really stupid right now."

BOOYAH. Yeah you do.

Long story short, he moved his things out.

I had already been doing a lot of personal growth before I met him, so I went into the mindset that it's not personal and had nothing to do with me. "Forgive and it will be easier for you," I told myself.

What I failed to do, however, was let myself feel what I wanted to feel. All my friends wondered why I wasn't mad and how I could be civil with him when our paths crossed. Then the emotion finally hit me - no kidding - almost a year later.

I was PISSED.

The first word that popped into my mind was, "coward." What kind of adult has such a lack of integrity that he can't tell the truth to someone's face?

At the time there was a silly app that was popular. It allowed you to anonymously "rate" ex-boyfriends. Completely ridiculous. The app was connected to Facebook.

I looked at it and said to my friends, "He's not showing up on my phone."

My friend pulled hers up.

"I can see him on mine. He must have blocked you."

I asked her to give me her phone and I saw he had some other questionable reviews from women.

There went my rampage. I honestly can't remember exactly what I wrote, but hitting that "post" button was more satisfying than popping a gigantic pimple.

(By the way, I am extremely fair when I write reviews and letters of recommendation - I only tell the truth.)

Was that the best thing I could have done? Probably not. But I also don't regret it. As far as I'm aware the app isn't around anymore. You live and you learn, and karma takes care of itself.

DESPITE THE HURT, I AM THANKFUL FOR THE EXPERIENCE.

It helped open a big wound for me. It wasn't that I wanted to be with him. The emotions surrounding betrayal, feeling unimportant, and not "good enough" were dormant in me long before this experience, and they needed to come out eventually.

Many of my pent-up emotions came from childhood. For

example, feeling "not good enough?" For those who aren't familiar with traditional Asian parenting, it basically goes like this: Anything you do receives criticism, and even if it's done well, it can always be better. The story I believed about myself was: I'm not good enough.

The experience of being cheated on, while not pleasant, was a big turning point for me.

It cracked me open and sparked a huge healing process, allowing me to do the work and show up how I wanted to for myself and my future partner. I did not want to suppress or ignore my pain. I wanted to work through it because if you don't, it comes back to haunt you.

I'm much more self-aware now, and because I healed a lot of my "stories," I was able to show up and create the relationship of my dreams with an amazing partner!

What I also learned from this experience: Self love, feel what you need to feel, and trust your goddamn gut.

A WOUND INHERITED FROM GENERATIONS

My grandparents fled to Vietnam when Japan invaded Guang Zhou, China during World War II.

My grandpa went first to get things settled. He hopped on a boat from Hong Kong to Saigon to start their new life and told my grandma to come meet him in a month.

One month later my grandma got on a boat to leave China with their first child (my dad's oldest brother). When she arrived at Saigon Harbor, baby in arms, she looked around. Her husband was nowhere in sight.

1939. Scared. Alone. In a new country. With a baby. And her husband didn't show up.

My dad told me she held onto that until the day she died.

It turns out my grandpa was busy working, so he sent a stranger to pick her up from the dock.

My grandpa wasn't a bad guy. He had a crazy work ethic, and I can't imagine what it was like having to flee from your country in 1939 to simply SURVIVE. But still, there's sadness when I tell that story. Good god, the first time I told that story to my therapist, the sobbing came out uncontrollably - so hard that I started to choke.

I felt her pain.

When I was growing up, even something as simple as waiting for hours for my parents to pick me up from grade school, it triggered pain. I was often the last kid on the playground. The worst was when it started to get dark. "Did they forget about me?" My parents ran their own business and were working all the time, so they would often forget or send one of their employees to pick me up. I felt unimportant.

A combination of experiences like this stack up so even today, if my husband does something that makes me angry, often the underlying reason is because I feel unimportant, and that my needs don't matter. It could be the littlest thing like him forgetting to deposit a check when I asked him to.

I *am* important. I *am* lovable. And what I say matters. He forgot to deposit the check because he forgot to deposit the check!

A lot of me is healed but these little "pain points" may never completely go away. It's like a muscle that constantly needs to be worked.

Like with any personal growth, you don't reach a certain destination and then not have to do the work anymore. It takes a lifetime of commitment to be your best self. Though I will say: it pays off ten-fold if you want to be happy and live your best life!

ACTION STEP:

Do you have any painful experiences like mine? What happened? Are you fully healed from it? Many of these pain points come from childhood and repeat themselves over and over. Maybe it was from past infidelity or other traumatic relationship heartbreak. Reflect on how it affected you. What stories did you make up about yourself?

- 4 -
Is There Something Wrong With Me?

My journey to meeting my husband felt like a long one. We didn't meet in our 20's like some of our other friends.

Time and again I wondered if something was wrong with me. Why didn't I have the luck other people had? Online dating was sometimes good and other times a nightmare. If it was "good," those relationships did not last.

I thought to myself: *I have a successful career, I'm good at a lot of things, my friends love me, and I actually want a relationship, so why when people asked how my love life is going, my insides wanted to shrivel up?*

Finally I figured it out.

"Luck is what happens when preparation meets opportunity."
~Seneca

If you want to be in a kick-ass relationship, you have to be ready to show up.

And by ready I mean:

- You actually want to be in a relationship.
- You feel good about yourself wherever you are in life.

YOU ATTRACT WHAT YOU ARE READY FOR

I could have potentially met my husband earlier in life, but the reason I didn't was simply because I wasn't prepared for it. "It" being the quality of relationship I wanted.

During this time, I photographed weddings for a living. No surprise I was drawn to this profession! I was drawn to LOVE, and this way I constantly got to see living examples of the type of relationship I wanted.

With each wedding I took mental notes:

- "Quiet comfort - I want that..."

- "A good community of friends and family - I want that..."

- "Being mean to each other in front of others - I definitely DO NOT want that..."

The kind of relationship I wanted: Easy. A partnership. Friendship. Mutual support. A lighthearted spirit. Both partners being generous and exuding mutual respect toward one another. Playful, self-expressed banter.

"I want a love like that..." is the order I put into the universe, and you know what the universe told me through my dating experiences?

You aren't ready to create that. If you want that, *this* is the person you have to become, meaning I couldn't expect someone to be open, vulnerable, emotionally intelligent, a good communicator, happy with themselves, to have done the "work" with minimal baggage... if I haven't fully done these things myself.

You attract what you are ready for.

Some people say they want a good relationship but won't show up, aka do what it takes, to create one. I was clear I wanted one, and I was willing to do whatever work I had to do on myself to show up as the version of me that felt good.

IT DEFINITELY DIDN'T HAPPEN OVERNIGHT

It took years of dating, personal growth, and learning to become the person I wanted to be, in order to create the relationship I wanted. Lessons came and repeated themselves over and over (and over) (and OVER) until I got fed up with my patterns and was **ready to do things differently.**

That's the good thing about getting frustrated and hitting lows - you get really sick of feeling a certain away, enough to finally take action.

I remember the moment I was DONE with my pattern of dating emotionally unavailable men (one of my patterns). I was sitting on my couch frustrated, snot-crying, and literally said, "I AM SICK OF FEELING THIS WAY." I threw myself back on the couch to be super dramatic, like in the movies. My friend was sitting next to me and his eyes opened wide as if to say, "Dude, are you ok?"

Insanity is doing the same thing over and over again, expecting a different result.

I've heard that quote so many times to the point it's annoying, but it's true. I was showing up repeatedly in a way that was attracting the wrong people and it was NOT working.

It was a hard pill for me to swallow that relationships were simply something I was not good at, so I decided that I wanted to learn and practice.

- 5 -

Career Success ≠
Relationship Success

My parents are immigrants from Vietnam and Cambodia. I learned a lot watching them work hard to build their business so that we could have a better life. It gave me a lot of confidence with work because they showed me what is possible with some grit and determination.

Therefore business comes naturally to me. When I was six, I put a little yellow table outside on the sidewalk to sell my drawings for 25 cents. After that, together with my sister and neighbors, we started a car wash at our home. I was the one coming up with campaign slogans, making marketing material, and leading the show. I had a lot of confidence producing things!

As an adult, it used to confuse me when creatives would come to me for business advice. They would ask things like, "A client wrote back and said they don't like my work. I'm devastated! How do you put yourself out there and charge what you charge?"

Whaaaaa? You just do it and put your work out there. If they don't want to hire you, it doesn't mean anything about you. Take it as feedback and improve where needed. Someone could literally bash my photography and it wouldn't mean anything to me because no matter what they say, I think my work is truly good! That person simply has different preferences.

My goal with dating was to feel how I felt with business. Confident. Easy. Not personal. Like I deserve it and am worthy of the best kind of love.

Confirming beliefs: What you believe to be true is what you'll hear. I learned about this from my therapist.

For example, say you post a photo on social media. Ten people will comment that you look beautiful, but one person will say you look terrible. If at the core you believe you are beautiful, the one troll comment won't affect you. But if deep down you believe you are not attractive, you will ignore the ten positive comments and focus on the one bad one, wondering if it's true.

My goal was to feel good in my romantic life so my confidence wouldn't be completely destroyed by someone else's choice or actions. I used to get CRUSHED if someone didn't show up the way I hoped because I made it mean something about me. To me, feeling bummed or disappointed was completely normal because it means you are able to be vulnerable, which is healthy. But I didn't like the feeling of letting someone else dictate my self-esteem. Someone not choosing me means I'm not good enough?

It was time to work on that.

- 6 -
You Are Not Alone

One year I was at an "exclusive" conference. It was one of those events where you have to get invited to go - the kind of conference an Overachiever loves to attend!

At this conference there were different talks on topics ranging from Internet Marketing to Fitness to Relationships.

The conference host asked, "Who has trouble with love and would like to learn more about building a healthy relationship?"

I looked around and almost the entire room of 150 people reluctantly raised their hands.

Phew, it's not just me.

You are not alone.

It's not uncommon that hard working, independent, driven people have a belief that makes them successful – the belief that there is always more to achieve, more to do, more to accomplish. Things are never good enough, and it's what makes them excel. While good for business and getting things done, it's not always the best for relationships.

If you are a successful, hard-working, and driven woman, yet you struggle to find love - you're in good company. And you're definitely not alone.

- 7 -
Why Take My Advice?

I'm not a certified relationship expert.

I'm a career woman sharing the story of how I struggled with relationships for most of my life, and how I learned to create the relationship of my dreams through personal growth. I hope my story can help you feel less alone and inspire you to make the changes you want to make.

I used to get anxiety when dating, hoping love would work out to the point of not wanting to check my phone in fear of disappointment that I didn't get a text or call from someone. If I was into a person and it didn't work out, I would be devastated.

Some people get disappointed after a breakup, but then they move forward. That was not me. Breakups unleashed a river of pain. I got depressed and made it all about me and why I'm not good enough. It felt like hopeless failure, which is not something I was used to in my career.

After lots of introspection, I learned about the stories I had created surrounding intimate relationships. It was not a positive narrative. I realized I had been playing small - focusing on the end goal - a successful relationship - and not the process of discovering who I was and what I needed.

I chose to do work on myself because I wanted to. I wanted to feel good. I wanted to shine in this area of my life.

It took years for me to heal past emotional trauma. During this time I also learned how to communicate in a healthy way, how to genuinely have FUN dating, be less afraid to be vulnerable, and not take it personally if nothing came out of it.

I went from letting other people choose me, to me choosing other people. I became confident in an area of my life that, as much as I hated to admit, l lacked complete self-confidence in.

I learned to love myself.

So much change happened during my personal growth years that one day I got rejected and actually felt GOOD that I had tried my best. Holy shit, I had the courage to put myself out there, communicate what I was feeling, *and* feel good about it? Go me!

Because do you know what playing small is costing you? It's costing you the relationship of your dreams.

- 8 -
Are You Stepping Up To Bat?

After doing personal growth for a few years and still feeling frustrated, I wondered if things would ever change. Then I met a guy named Greyson.

Greyson and I went back and forth liking each other for years and had this cute, stupid dynamic where every time we were around each other, we'd both become really shy.

We always hung out as friends, and eventually I developed a huge crush on him, though I didn't want to say anything for fear of rejection. Also, in my head I always thought it would be more romantic if the guy made the first move. Not true!

Finally one night I picked up the phone and called him. Not gonna lie, it was awkward as fuck because I wasn't used to talking like this, but I knew letting things organically happen between us wasn't working. We had literally tip-toed around each other for years.

It was night time and we had just finished hanging out at a bar with mutual friends. I started to drive home and hated that I just hugged him bye like we were friends. I pulled over because it was a now or never moment. I got my phone out to call him.

"Hey!" I said awkwardly.

"Hey..." he said with a confused tone.

I don't remember fully what I said but it was along the lines of "I like you and would like to hang out as more than just friends. Can we do that?"

I must have said it with my eyes closed tight, barely able to breathe. *Good god. He's going to reject me solely based on how awkward I said it,* I thought.

Do you know what he said?

"CC, I can't believe you are telling me this because I've liked you for so long and I didn't think you liked me back in that way. Yes I'd love to."

Logic here. *Ding dong!* If I can't tell or show someone I like them, I'm not even giving them a chance. This was the part of me that was scared to be vulnerable.

Could he have said no? Of course. In which case I would have been super bummed, but at least I went up to bat. If it was a no, it would free up space for me to move on.

Greyson was very cute and sweet, and he was right for me in that moment of my life. I learned a lot about myself during this time because he and I were so emotionally similar that it kind of felt like I was dating...myself.

Huh, so that's what I'm like.

I'm happy we dated, even though he did crush my heart into a million pieces at the time we broke up. He didn't want to take things further when I did, but he was (and still is!) a good person. We weren't on the same page, and after mourning it, I came to accept that.

Are you taking risks and putting yourself out there? Are you showing up, even when it means being vulnerable? Don't close yourself off to possibility because you're afraid to act.

- 9 -
My Worst Nightmare Realized

Some of my worst nightmares have included:

- Getting attacked by a great white shark.

- Having orange juice spilled on my lap during a flight, leaving me sitting wet and sticky for hours.

- Drowning.

- Having a bot fly lay eggs under my skin and it hatching (Ugh!).

- My ex dating someone new right after we break up.

- Getting stuck on a dark scary ride at Disneyland by myself and no one noticing, leaving me to spend the night in there alone with all the Animatronics still running until the morning shift comes in.

- Wearing open-toe sandals on an escalator and then one of my toes getting caught and popping off.

Only one of these things has actually happened - I bet you can guess which one.

I used to be terrified that an ex who broke my heart would start dating someone new right after we broke up. It bothered me because I thought it meant I'm not good enough ("Is she prettier?"), I did something wrong ("I shouldn't have done that one thing"), I failed ("Why can't I be in a relationship like everyone else?"), or simply that I felt betrayed.

For much of my dating life, breakups felt like the worst thing that could possibly happen. *Especially* if he moved on right away.

With time, the pain went away after each breakup. The truth is that some exes used to trigger things within me even if I didn't really want to be with them. Along with the list of qualities I wanted in a partner like integrity, empathy, etc., I wanted someone who was excited to be with me. I deserve that!

Now that I've seen my exes date other girls (even shortly after we broke up), what I feared is not scary anymore. I learned that their actions after our breakup had nothing to do with me.

So to those exes, I say, "Good luck sir. I bid you adieu."

Then!... I hear through the grapevine that his life has blown up in flames because he still has the same patterns with EVERY romantic partner he's ever had, which in the long run bites him in the ass.

I knew it. *slow satisfying grin*

I'm joking, but let's be real. Not really.

But let's just say things *did* work out well and the ex marries the new girl. He is who he is, and now he has a partner who is ok with his qualities. ALL of them.

- 10 -
Self-Awareness Is Key

So how do you get there? To the point when you can say "I bid you adieu" without gritting your teeth and silently cursing him?

The answer is self-awareness. Self-awareness to know what you need to heal and move forward.

If you want things to change, this will take a commitment to yourself.

People like to focus on the qualities of who they're dating, but it's more important to know yourself than the other person. If you know yourself really well, you will know when you've met the right match.

Through self-awareness you will learn what you want versus what you need, how to communicate what you need, what your boundaries are, areas you may still need to heal, and what changes you may need to make to create your ideal relationship.

If you ignore getting to know yourself and choose a partner based solely on charm, pheromones, and sexy lighting, you might hop into a relationship for the wrong reason and commit to someone who isn't a good long-term fit.

So kudos for making the effort to get to know yourself better because when the time comes, you will choose a partner who you are crazy about AND who is a good fit for you.

Learning about yourself can sometimes be painful, disappointing, and scary. On the flipside it can also be heartwarming and liberating. Having self-awareness and a good relationship with yourself truly is the foundation you need in order to build a good relationship with someone else.

ACTION STEP:

Look in the mirror. Do you genuinely
like the person you are looking at?

- 11 -
What Does Your Best Look Like?

A good gauge for self-awareness is knowing what it feels like when you're at your best, and what it feels like when you aren't.

For me, when I feel good:

- I have a lot of energy.
- I'm self-expressive.
- I talk a lot.
- I laugh a lot
- I'm not bothered by the actions of others.
- I am physically fit.
- I'm inspired with work.
- I get tons of ideas.
- I sleep well.

When I don't feel good:

- I feel drained and disconnected.
- I'm insecure.
- I criticize others.
- I'm annoyed by other people.
- I eat badly.

- I feel drawn to watch true crime shows and other depressing things.

- I'm tempted to buy expensive things to fill a void.

- I grind my teeth at night.

ACTION STEP:

Take a few moments to
brainstorm your own lists.

What does it look like when you
feel good (aka your BEST)?

What does it look like when
you do not feel good?

- 12 -
The Intimidation Factor

When I was in college, my dad told me that a lot of guys would feel inadequate dating me because I had already traveled to so many places in the world.

He said, "He's going to take you to Vegas and feel ridiculous."

I told him I don't care where they take me - that they don't have to take me anywhere. He said it didn't matter, that they will still feel that way.

I've also had friends tell me that guys will be intimidated by me for similar reasons. "You're independent and travel a lot. A lot of guys aren't comfortable with that."

While it may be true that some men get intimidated, a lot of them also LOVE ambitious go-getter women.

"For the right person your independence won't intimidate them, it will turn them on." ~Mark Groves, Human Connection Specialist

After I met Pete, I continued to travel. I even went to the UK for three months right after we met because I always wanted to spend an extended period of time overseas.

Eventually I asked him, "Do you genuinely feel ok with me traveling this much and doing my own thing?"

He said, "Babe, that's why I chose you. You're independent and confident doing your own thing."

He doesn't deal with my independence, he loves and encourages it. Pete was clear on what he wanted when I met him. He wasn't one of those guys who says, "I want an ambitious woman," but when one shows up they can't handle it. Pete knew himself and meant what he said.

After we got to know each other better, I realized Pete indeed would not do well with someone who is unambitious or who didn't have their "own thing." He can be independent too. He has his guy friends, soccer, and hobbies he loves to do to wind down from work. He wanted a partner who understands and is happy letting him do his own thing too, because they live life in a similar fashion. And hey! That's me!

If you find a man is intimidated by you and prefers his partner to play smaller, that's fine. He's not for you. Let him find someone who doesn't intimidate him, and you can find someone who is drawn to your ambition and skills. That's it. No more to it.

- 13 -
Breaking Patterns

If there is any kind of repetitive result in your life, it's not other people, it's you.

Some of my dating patterns have included choosing people who were not emotionally available and choosing people who made me feel abandoned.

"The brain likes what is familiar." ~Marisa Peer, Rapid Transformational Therapy Trainer

If you keep choosing people who make you feel a certain way, it's because that feeling is familiar. So train yourself to be in the unfamiliar.

Breaking patterns takes time. Something immediate you can do is start with little things. How you are in one area of your life affects all other areas, no matter how seemingly small.

For example, one time I bought a bubble gum pink shirt because I NEVER wear pink. My typical way of dressing is like a Parisian - simple and timeless with neutral colors. The pink shirt...when I put it on I felt like a different person. When I walked into my office wearing it for the first time, the people who were used to seeing me in my neutral work uniform said, "Look at you. You look nice!"

Not to say I looked crappy before, but I thought it was interesting how they picked up on an energy shift in me that day. **New** energy. **Different** energy!

Another simple thing I've done to facilitate breaking patterns is changing my workout routine. Recently I took some Hollywood stunt classes. These classes teach you martial arts, fight sequences, flying on wires, etc.

Do I want to be a stunt actor? No. But it is forcing my body to move in new ways. It's different from my regular workout routine. It also involves choreography, so it's good for the brain. And doing fight sequences on wires? I'm living out my Crouching Tiger, Hidden Dragon dreams!

Dive into the unfamiliar. If you usually eat your eggs sunny side up, scramble them.

Of course, what would be most effective is breaking patterns with bigger things, like if you are a people-pleaser, begin saying no to people when they overstep your boundaries.

It'll feel awkward, scary, and unfamiliar at first, but that's the only way to begin change. Start doing things **differently**.

ACTION STEP:

To get used to the unfamiliar, what are three small things that you will start to do differently tomorrow?

Are You Open Though?

After I had been cheated on and started learning more about myself, I regularly went to see a life coach named Gypsy. He was an older Native American man with long black and grey hair. He was wise, direct, and no BS.

During one visit, he asked what I wanted in a partner.

Me: "Someone who wants a relationship too. Someone who's crazy about me and grateful for what he has."

Gypsy: "If he showed up right now would you be ready for him?"

Me: "Yes. I want a relationship."

Gypsy: Pauses like he wants to say something, but instead smiles and says, "Ok..."

(Translation: "Hell no you aren't.")

At that time, if a guy showed up ready, it would freak me the F out. I wasn't ready for that level of intimacy. My heart was closed because of past hurts.

Today I have the same conversation with some of my single friends that Gypsy had with me. They say they are open, yet when they meet someone who actually shows up and calls them, they run. Or they'll criticize something trivial about a guy that has nothing to do with what they say they want.

"I don't like lawyers."

"His hairline though."

"I don't like guys from LA."

You've never even met the person - how do you know you won't like them? Is your judgment based on previous experience? Is this new person going to be exactly like the last person you've dated who happened to have a trivial characteristic in common? Is he triggering a past trauma in you, causing you to shut down?

I can't tell you how many people I've met who say something like, "I only like Asians" but eventually end up marrying a Caucasian, or vice versa.

If you're open you'll literally SEE more opportunity and may start to find things attractive that you didn't before. You might even fall in love with your best guy friend who's secretly been in love with you since you met.

Remember to stay open. You aren't committing to being with someone you feel "eh" about. All you are doing is trying new things.

Begin saying, "I would normally say no to going out with someone like this, but I'll try it out."

Approach it with curiosity. Learn more about yourself. Stay open, honest, and available.

WHAT IF? WHEN STAYING OPEN LEADS TO FIREWORKS.

At Peter & Catherine's wedding, Peter stood up to make a speech. I was at this wedding photographing it.

He told the story of their first date and how at the end of it, Catherine blew him off nicely by saying, "I think we would make really great *friends*."

He went home bummed. He really liked her and had just been

friend-zoned. He called his sister and close friends. They encouraged him to keep pursuing her, so he got the courage to ask her out again. She agreed. She stayed open to possibility.

On their second date, there were sparks.

Two years later, they were married.

At the end of his wedding speech Peter looked at Catherine and said, "Catherine, thank you for giving us a chance."

I wiped tears as I kept taking pictures.

It got me thinking how BIG our seemingly little life decisions are. What if Peter didn't muster up the courage to ask her out again? What if Catherine decided to say no to the second date? Then he wouldn't be looking at her, giving that speech, on their wedding day.

It was a reminder to have the courage to go after what you want in life. Be open. The worst thing you can get is a no. The best thing you can get is, well, who knows??

- 15 -

Pay Attention To What You Want

I became drawn to photographing weddings because it put me around relationships of all sorts – mothers, daughters, besties, grandparents, coworkers, and of course – lovers.

Witnessing intimate moments at hundreds of weddings has helped me become clear on what I wanted in a partner, but more importantly how I need to show up in order to create the relationship of my dreams. These are some of the moments that helped me recognize mine had shown up.

LET YOUR FREAK FLAG FLY

Dina was one of the most radiant brides I've ever seen. She's loud, hilarious, and says what's on her mind. She lets her "freak flag" fly wherever she goes, and guess what? Her husband adores that about her. In a lot of the photos I took her husband is looking at her endearingly while she's doing something hilarious.

I spent a good chunk of my life feeling like I couldn't be 100% me without feeling judged, so I knew I wanted a partner who not only accepts, but adores me for being 100% me.

LOVE ME FOR ME

After the wedding ceremony, Danny told Maggi, "I LOVE that dress. It's so... (*he smiles)... you."

He didn't love the dress because he has a thing for a particular style. He loved it because she chose it, and because he loves her. Likewise, I wanted a partner who loves me for me. Also, I adored the way he looked at her. Not only on their wedding day, but all the time. I still stalk them on social media sometimes.

MUTUAL GRATITUDE

When Tim saw Liz for the first time as a bride during their "First Look," he broke down and embraced her for a full minute, digging his face into her neck.

Then he looked at me while I was snapping photos and said, "Do you see how lucky I am?"

Inserted into mental piggy bank: someone who is grateful for me, as I am equally for them.

FRIENDSHIP = EASE

Annie and Jon were best friends. They never told me that, but you could see it. They had a relaxed comfort whether they were interacting together or existing quietly side-by-side. Things were...easy.

I learned one of the most important things to me in a relationship is ease, and having a partner who is also a friend.

MUTUAL RESPECT AND ACKNOWLEDGEMENT

This wasn't at a wedding, but at a weekend in Sedona with friends. Dean and Lisa have been married over twenty years and have a daughter together. It was cold one night, and he was outside BBQing.

He came in and asked his wife, "Honey, could you come outside and help me?"

She said in the most gentle tone, "Of course!," and eagerly rushed outside to help him.

It's simple dialogue, but the way they speak to each other always involves mutual respect and acknowledgment.

I didn't see that growing up so I was drawn to it, and to this day I try my best to practice presence and respect with my husband. Of course we have moments where our emotions get the best of us (mostly me, I'm the fiery one!), but having a blueprint like Dean and Lisa's marriage is inspiring, and has made an impact on how I want to show up.

It makes a difference when you get to be around living examples of the kind of relationship you want. Some people don't think a certain kind of love is possible, and I think that's because they have never experienced or seen it before. I feel lucky to be around these kinds of moments all the time.

ACTION STEP:

Seek out examples of relationships you admire, and take mental (or actual!) notes. Store up ideas of what you want - and don't want - from real-life couples around you.

- 16 -
It's Not Always Rainbows And Butterflies

In addition to the good stuff, what was helpful for me was talking about the challenging parts of relationships with people who were in marriages that I admired. It's important to hang with people who will share the struggles too because we all have them, no matter how good it looks from the outside.

I wanted to know: How do they navigate life together when things get tough?

My friend Leslie has a marriage I admire very much, and she was a huge role model for me before I met Pete. Her husband is a sexy successful actor and he ADORES her to death.

She told me that their marriage hit a rough patch about seven years in, but not once would she say, "He did this...this... and that...and he never does this... this...and that."

Instead she said, "When we hit a rough patch I went to counseling, took workshops, and did everything I could."

Leslie is a strong woman. She has great boundaries and self-respect while being one of the most generous people I know. She takes responsibility for herself and works on herself first before attacking or blaming. I always remember that.

One time she also told me that she and her husband don't talk philosophically much. Leslie LOVES philosophy and can ramble about it all day. She said they both admit that it would be nice if they had that interest in common, but it wasn't a deal breaker. In addition to her marriage, I saw that Leslie created an amazing community of friends, and that's where she talks philosophy!

This was the first time I realized you don't need one person to check every single box of what you think you want to have a fantastic marriage.

- 17 -
Timing Matters

I sometimes think: what if I married someone I dated in my 20's or early 30's? Good god. Dodged a bullet with that one.

While some of the guys I dated were fun and had great qualities, they weren't the best match for me based on what I need emotionally.

I'm grateful I met Pete at a point in my life when I became a lot more clear on my values, beliefs, and what I emotionally need (because that was almost always missing from my previous partners). I stayed open, and we met each other when we were both ready.

Is it possible that things are not aligning with someone you click with, but they could mature down the road and then be "ready" for you? I like to be optimistic and say anything is possible. The question is: *do you want to wait and see?*

I dated a guy before Pete who I really liked and who I thought could have been a great match, though he was in a place where he felt unsure about what he wanted. By then I had reached a point where I did not want to wait around for anyone anymore. I wanted someone who felt sure about me (because I felt sure about me!).

People can only change if they want to, and even if they do change, everyone is on their own timing. You can't force that.

So I did not wait. I trusted that if I continued to do my own thing and stayed open to whatever came, I would receive the relationship I wanted. A few weeks later I met Pete.

- 18 -
The Moment I Knew

The first time I looked into Pete's eyes, I had a hunch. He was handsome, and I could tell he was kind, gentle, mature, and trusting. When I looked at him, I felt interested, curious, and calm. Not raging OMFG butterflies when your logical thinking goes out the door, but like a feeling of home. I knew it was worth exploring.

At that time in my dating life I wasn't surprised when a guy failed to show up the way I needed him to, but time and time again, Pete surprised me by going above and beyond.

A couple months in, I was at his place. My sister called and told me my dad had a heart attack. My family lives in San Francisco while I'm in LA. My dad was in the hospital recovering.

I laid down in bed and turned away on my side to face the wall. I didn't expect him to do anything, or even worse, I thought he would back away. Almost every guy I dated before him was uncomfortable with vulnerability or intimacy.

But Pete laid down next to me, spooned me, and after a couple minutes of silence said, "You know, I often feel guilty that I live far from home and don't get to see my family much."

My body relaxed and my held-back tears poured out. That's when I knew.

He's got me.

- 19 -
More On Healing

Some people have made the comment after meeting me a couple times that they like my confidence.

Uhhh....

What they haven't seen are the rampant thoughts that run through my head, the times I'm socially nervous (it's usually one-on-one with someone I don't know well), and the times I have breakdowns and want to stay in bed.

Everyone has healing to do no matter how confident they appear from the outside. I had to heal and let go of a lot of my emotional stories before being able to show up confidently in my romantic life.

I do a lot of personal growth in general (even to this day) because how I function at the core affects how I show up in all areas of my life. Not to mention, my #1 goal in life is to be happy and healthy. If I'm good in that area, I don't care what my external circumstances are.

As you dive into your personal growth journey, a question you can ask yourself:

What happened to you that affected your confidence and self-worth in your romantic life?

- Maybe your parents told you you weren't good enough.
- Maybe a teacher said you'd never amount to anything.
- Maybe someone cheated on you.
- Maybe you blamed yourself for the end of your last

relationship and called yourself a failure.

- Maybe someone told you you don't deserve good things and have to earn them.

- Maybe no one did anything to you, and you made up the stories that you are no good on your own.

I don't know what happened to you, but it's your job to figure out where the stories come from so you can understand them and let them go.

Some of my old stories:

- I'm not good enough.

- There's something wrong with me.

- I'm not important.

- I shouldn't inconvenience other people.

- It's up to other people to choose me.

- I'm lucky if they choose me.

- I don't deserve great love.

- I'm stupid.

- People will like me if I am accomplished.

Healing takes time. Be patient and gentle with yourself. My self-talk is naturally critical because of how I was spoken to as a child.

It takes consistent practice to shift to a positive narrative. And by consistent I mean hanging out with positive, supportive people and saying nice things to myself everyday until it became a habit.

It also means still going to self-improvement retreats and seeing a therapist when I feel I need it. I do my best to not bottle things up, but breaking childhood habits is a forever work in progress. I like to check in and make sure I'm doing the best I can.

The thing I've learned from coaching others is that you can't coach yourself. You need a team of people who can support you. Intellectually you may understand what you need to do, but involving others who can see clearly and without bias will get you there faster.

HOW DID I HEAL?

Different things work for different people.

I'm someone who likes to try new things, so I've tried it all. I even had a "shaman" (who was clearly born in California but gave herself a long spiritual name) hum lyrics and spit water on me. In case anyone is wondering, it did not work. Be open and curious, remember?

I know I respond best to direct advice and not being coddled, but I also learned something new: Despite my tough exterior, I need to be given a safe space where I can acknowledge the parts of me that were hurt.

BUT WHAT DO *YOU* NEED?

You may need different things at different times. Try different strategies to see what works for you. Below are things I have done that helped with healing.

TALK ABOUT IT

Some people find it embarrassing to talk about their struggles with love. I didn't actively talk about it unless someone I trusted asked, and they would really have to pry.

One time I was hanging out with my friend Dawn.

Out of nowhere she asked, "We've never talked about this, but what's going on in your love life? What's the story you have associated with it?"

I had hung out with her at several conferences, and she knew me well enough to know something was holding me back.

My story at the time was: *I don't know if I can have what I want. A guy who has all the qualities I want. I'm attracted to him and he's loyal to me - does it even exist?*

She looked at me with wide eyeballs as I was talking and said, "Oh my god, that is completely made up in your head. We are surrounded by fantastic guys all the time - you see them at the conferences, you've met your friends' husbands... they're great guys!"

Hearing her say that was reassuring. The logical side of me knew I was making up stories, but having someone else say it to me, and with such confidence, felt good.

You know what else felt good? It was just in my mind, which meant, I can change this! The "truth" I had been telling myself wasn't actually true.

SEE A THERAPIST

For years I made fun of people who saw a therapist. "Damn. These people are messed up," is what I thought.

I was so, so wrong.

People who see a therapist are strong enough to acknowledge they need help and support. Also, they aren't ashamed to get it.

My therapist helped me see things that I didn't know bothered me.

For example, one of the things she asked me during our first meeting was, "Are your parents together or divorced?"

I said divorced. I've made this statement hundreds of times since I was twelve without flinching. It was matter-of-fact and I was always fine with it, or so I thought.

As soon as I said, "They're divorced," she sat back, looked at me, and waited for me to say more.

She gave me a safe space. Ten seconds later tears poured down my face and I looked down.

"I didn't know that bothered me," I said to her.

Stemming from that, I realized there was hurt associated with my dad.

This was tough because I've always been a daddy's girl. My dad is the funniest man I know and has always let me be who I am. I love him to death for it.

However, there were things he has done that were out of integrity, and I realized through therapy that it upset me. I wrote him a letter because I wanted him to know the impact that his actions can have. It wasn't to criticize him. I didn't need him to say anything or do anything - I just wanted him to know that it hurt me. Sending it was healing.

The next time I saw him I felt empowered, and I was just as happy to see him as I was before.

I could tell he was emotional and he even said, "I don't know why I'm so emotional right now. I'm sorry," as he hugged me.

Without therapy, I never would have had these breakthroughs.

DO PERSONAL GROWTH CLASSES AND WORKSHOPS

My favorite courses helped me improve my communication tremendously and let go of personal stories that held me back in all areas of my life.

Upon taking them, I learned I prefer a direct logical approach because it was how I was spoken to growing up. Often when people are talking to me, I'm wishing for them to get to the point already!

But that is not for everyone.

If someone is depressed, not an independent thinker, or emotionally fragile, a direct logical approach may not be the best way to learn. You can't tell a fragile person facts that are x, y, z while they are having a panic attack. They may prefer being spoken to in a more gentle way that gets to the point 20 sessions later so they have time to process.

The best way to figure out what's right for you is to start trying different things and see which you love and which repulse you. Uncomfortable is good because it means you are growing, repulsion is not.

GET A LIFE COACH

I've spoken to many life coaches, but Gypsy was my favorite. I heard about him through someone I worked with.

She said, "I went to see this man named Gypsy – he is trained in 67 different healing techniques. It was life changing. You'll look at yourself in the mirror after a session with him and literally see yourself differently."

She was right. Gypsy was intuitive and after five minutes of talking to me he knew my "issues" and how they manifested in my life and my body.

He said, "Someone like you tends to have physical ailments in this region of your body (motions to my groin, bladder, etc.) because you don't let things go."

He was right about it all, and my favorite thing about him was that he didn't talk for hours. He asked the right questions and was to the point. He cracked my back where it needed to be cracked, made me scream into pillows, and told me to cut the bullshit every time I went to see him.

He suggested things to do but never told me I should or shouldn't do something. It was exactly what I needed.

JUST SAY NO TO DING DONGS

After knowing Gypsy for a couple years and talking about my dating life (for the 50th time), he said, "What are you doing dating these Mickey Mouse Ding Dongs?"

- Because I'm afraid there might be nothing else out there for me.
- Because I feel I don't deserve something great when it comes to love.
- Because I have shitty boundaries with things that actually matter.
- Because I think they will change.
- Because I think I can fix them.
- Because I'm scared of intimacy and being seen.
- Because I'm scared of being alone forever.

These insights came to me after years of personal growth and actively seeking answers.

Find what you need and what works for you. When you learn to take care of what you need, you set a higher standard of what to expect from others.

Today I treat myself so well that there isn't anyone who can treat me better. I love my husband but he can't be in my head 24/7. Even when he does thoughtful things for me, it's different when you do them for yourself.

To this day I still take myself on trips, go to movies alone, sign up for retreats, and do things that light me up.

OTHER OPTIONS FOR PHYSICAL AND EMOTIONAL HEALING:

SPAS AND MASSAGES

Self care = self love. Touch is very important. When you are really vulnerable you tap into what you needed as a child. In LA we have Korean spas. The ladies scrub you down, wash your hair, tie your hair up, and wrap you up in a towel. I like it because it reminds me of how my mom bathed me when I was a kid. It's nurturing.

At other times you might want male physical energy. Now, this is not sexual. Unless you are into hiring someone for that, which, who am I to judge?

Having a male massage therapist does not mean you have to be attracted to the masseuse. It is simply being physically touched with masculine energy. If that sounds appealing to you, request a male massage therapist.

ACUPUNCTURE, CUPPING, REIKI, AYURVEDA, AND TRADITIONAL CHINESE MEDICINE

These are natural techniques for long term healing results. It doesn't cover things up nor is it a quick fix. Instead it goes to the source to help realign where you have blocks.

RELEASE RAGE

Have pent up anger? Some cities have "rage rooms" where they give you a baseball bat, club, crow bar, or weapon of choice, and you get to go into a room and break things.

The fact that a business like this exists means A LOT of people have pent up anger. No shame in it. Take care of yourself. One month I went twice. "You're back," they said. Yes, and I had a great time smashing that old computer.

SOUND BATHS

Sound changes energy. Even if you get nothing spiritual out of it, the least you'll get is the best nap of your life.

YOGA

Learn to BREATHE through discomfort. I do Vinyasa because I

like sweating my ass off as well as Kundalini, which involves a lot of breathing to balance your nervous system.

DISCOVER NEW PEOPLE & PLACES

There is a big world out there. When I get into the zone that "everything is about me," all I have to do is step outside and look at all the people around me. In my mind I create all these problems, and then I look at everyone else walking by and ask, "I wonder what's going on in their world?"

I found that going to a new place, whether local or far away, also works well for me because it makes it easy to see things with new eyes. Especially if a culture is very different from mine, it helps me see that my way is not the only way. Everyone is living their life according to what they think is right.

FIND A COMMUNITY

Find a community with a value system you like. It can be a church, an entrepreneurs group, a mom group, a martial arts gym, anything.

It's difficult to do life alone. A good positive community will hold you accountable and help you feel understood. Start talking to others. If you feel lonely it's because you don't feel connected (by the way it's possible to be around lots of people, talk to them, and not feel connected). Openness and vulnerability are important. Also, *"You are the average of the 5 people you spend the most time with," ~Jim Rohn*, so surround yourself with people you want to be like.

MOVE IN NEW WAYS

Do an activity that requires you to move in new ways. Moving in new ways changes energy. It's also great for self-expression and staying open. My favorite is dance.

Growing up I was trained in ballet and jazz. Hip hop is new for me, and even though I feel ridiculous doing it, I like that it's different from how I'm used to moving. I also like heels dance classes. No pole, just dancing sexy in heels.

THE MOST IMPORTANT THING, IF YOU WANT CHANGE, IS TO TRULY WANT IT AND TAKE ACTION

The only way to improve life and get results is to do something different. Try something. Anything! You'll learn something new or you'll hate it. At least you're taking initiative, and you're winning by simply learning about yourself.

As time goes on you'll discover what works for you and what doesn't. Maybe you prefer a coach who is soft and supportive and uses flowery language. Or maybe you respond better to someone who is direct, holds you accountable, and speaks bluntly. Most likely you will need different things at different times, so listen and be aware of that.

Also, remember to be patient and gentle with yourself. Change and growth take time. Did you build your career overnight? Unless you were an overnight sensation on YouTube or born into a prestigious family, you know it took years of long days, nights, countless mistakes, and perseverance.

If you want to create the relationship of your dreams, commit to yourself first.

ACTION STEP:

Reflect on the strategies I've listed.
What will spark healing for you?

Be open and start trying different
things. What do you have to lose?

- 20 -

THE REAL YOU:
Show Up To Dates As You Show Up With Your Friends

After a couple years of seeing my life coach Gypsy, he said, "I can't think of a reason a guy would not want to be with you... if you are showing up as the same person when you come meet with me."

That was the problem. I wasn't the same person when I went on dates and got into relationships. I became an unsure I'm-not-good-enough version of me. I was nervous and felt I had to do things to keep the other person interested.

The story I had for a long time was, "I'm not romantically lovable."

All my friends loved me, their husbands loved me, and my guy friends loved me. They liked the confident, opinionated, pain-in-the-ass version of me that didn't care what others thought.

It became clear that if I could show up as the "real me" when I dated, I would have this in the bag. Personal growth and trying new things helped me figure out who the "real me" actually was. My goal was to be authentic and consistent like that in all areas of my life. Work, friends, family, love life - all the same me.

Are you confident in knowing the real you? The real you is where you want to be, all the time.

- 21 -

TAPPING INTO YOUR SOFT SIDE:
Slowing Down To Find The Joy

"Water is fluid, soft, and yielding. But water will wear away rock, which is rigid and cannot yield. As a rule, whatever is fluid, soft, and yielding will overcome whatever is rigid and hard. This is another paradox: what is soft is strong." ~Lao Tzu

It's easier to say, "I'm pissed off" than "I'm hurt."

Tapping into my soft side brings me joy. When I do this, I stop swimming upstream. I receive. I nurture.

When I was younger I loved to bake and do arts and crafts.

As an adult I stopped doing those things and even looked down on them because I got too focused on the entrepreneur/manager mindset. "My time is precious - I have better things to do like make money."

Doing things like crafts brings me joy if I'm in a present headspace. In the moment. Process-oriented. Mindful. Not point A to point B. Have you ever roved a wool doll before? Pure joy.

I also really got into cooking and baking again after spending my first Christmas in New Jersey with my in-laws. Pete has a big family. His mom along with all his aunts and uncles cook together. They make cookies from recipes that were passed down from generations. Being in the kitchen with them reminded me to find joy in the process. There was also a lot of joy in eating all of it!

It's constant practice to be present and enjoy the process.

The other day I took the metro in LA with friends instead of hopping in my car. The car would have been faster, but I enjoyed the quality time with my friends.

The sun was setting so the light was warm and golden. We stopped to get iced mochas. I enjoyed getting to talk to my friends while on the metro without having to look at the road. We talked about me writing this book. They gave me feedback.

These habits make me an all around happier person because as long as I'm in the mindset of, "It'll be good someday..." I'll never be truly happy. If that's the case, after I accomplish whatever I wanted (getting to the destination, getting that promotion, meeting that person, booking that client), a new problem will arise for me to fix and be unhappy about.

I also want to acknowledge that feminine activities like baking or crafting don't produce happiness for everyone. If you don't like doing that stuff, don't do them! The most important thing is to **know what brings you joy**.

I keep a post-it taped to my laptop with a list of things that bring me joy (to remind myself on crappy days):

On my list:

- Trying new things
- Going to the dog park
- Traveling to new places
- Dance
- French cafes
- Disneyland
- Witty, funny people

Whenever I'm feeling down or stuck, I reference that post-it that is taped to my laptop. "Oh yeah, I can go to the dog park during lunch."

ACTION STEP:

Make your own list of things that bring
you joy and tape it somewhere you can see.
When you're feeling down or in a rut, choose
something from your list to find some joy.

- 22 -
Take Some Time To Daydream

Write a list of what you wish a partner would do with or for you.

Some things on my list:

- Go on adventures around the world
- Take me out to eat at awesome restaurants
- Be patient, gentle, and empathetic
- Have fun together
- Sneak burritos into the movie theater
- Buy me nice things
- Pamper me with spa treatments

Whatever is on your list, start doing those things for yourself. It might sound hokey and rah-rah but if you actually do it, over time it will start to feel really good!

Before I met Pete I took myself on adventurous trips to places like India, Micronesia, and the Cook Islands. Sometimes I would invite friends. If no one could go, I still went by myself.

You may learn that you prefer to go on trips with someone else, but that doesn't mean you can't still enjoy yourself. If you are a people person, join a group tour.

I learned how to make myself happy instead of waiting for someone to fill the void.

Anytime you put responsibility onto another person, you are setting yourself up to possibly be disappointed. But do you know who will always show up for you? That's right. You.

When you learn to stand on your own, any person who comes into your life will enhance it, not turn into a crutch. I like it this way because it's emotionally healthy and feels better. After all, the main goal really is to feel GOOD, no matter what the external circumstances look like.

- 23 -
Be Kind To Yourself

Imagine you are taking a new dance class. The movements are new and you have trouble picking up choreography. You start to feel frustrated and really want to nail it. You feel like you suck and start to get angry (I may be using a personal example).

First - it's a recreational dance class. Calm down.

Second - you getting angry at yourself is not treating yourself kindly. Imagine if there were someone on the sidelines getting annoyed and angry at you for not getting the choreo. That would be a shitty person. Wouldn't you want someone to be encouraging and supportive? Be that person for yourself. Instead say something to yourself like, "Good job for showing up and trying. You know how many people want to do this but are too scared to? Practice and you'll get better with time."

Be who you needed when you were younger. For me, I wanted someone patient and supportive.

Be who you want on the sidelines.

ACTION STEP:

What did the kid version of you need? What did support look like to you as a child?

Lessons From My Dog

My old dog had surgery on her paw. She couldn't climb up stairs wearing the cone-of-shame, so I began to carry her.

Three weeks later the cone-of-shame was removed, bandages off. She went back to running around and attacking dogs on the street.

One night at 4:00am she started crying at the bottom of the stairs. I stayed curled up half asleep in my upstairs bedroom. More crying.

I yelled, "Sammie, stop it. If you can attack another dog, I know you can climb the stairs."

She continued to cry.

Pillow over my head. It didn't work. I grumpily got out of bed and went downstairs. There she was, spinning in circles, tongue hanging out. I carried her up. She hopped in bed and burrowed under the sheets.

I knew this would start happening. I had trained her to rely on me to carry her up the stairs and in return, she trained me to continue doing it.

We train everyone in our lives how to treat us. If there is someone in your life who treats you poorly, it's because you've taught them that what they are doing is acceptable.

If you have a bunch of takers in your life, it's because you allow them to take without contributing anything back. If you don't like that someone always runs late and doesn't respect your time, it's because you allow them to be late. The people who show up in your life are a result of your own behavior and actions.

My dog is smart. She has trained me well.

ACTION STEP:

How are you "training" the people in
your life? Are there boundaries you
need to enforce or loosen up?

- 25 -

RESILIENCE

Noun, The Capacity To Recover Quickly From Difficulties; Toughness

My friend called me and said she felt hurt because her boss chose someone else to lead a project instead of her. It hurt her feelings enough to make her cry.

She went into all the reasons she is more qualified for the job, how the other person has made many mistakes in the past, etc.

I asked, "Details aside, have you experienced this before? Maybe not in work but in personal life? Someone choosing someone else instead of you?"

I already knew the answer because I've known her since college.

She said, "Yes. I need to work on my self-worth. I hate feeling undervalued."

I've always had a lot of confidence in my professional life, but where I could relate to her was in romantic relationships.

For years I was devastated if I was rejected. I felt not good enough, like I was doing something wrong, and that others were better than me. It triggered an emotional cord where I would literally sabotage relationships because of my lack of self-confidence in that area.

Deep down I knew I wanted a good relationship, and I did not want to settle.

The healing work was the most profound for me. When you heal, you become clear and build confidence.

At times it felt like things wouldn't change. Years went by and I still felt devastated every time I got rejected. Lots of frustration.

Fast forward a couple years. I was dating someone new.

It started off casual – we both wanted to keep it light. But at this point I was clear that I wanted to create a committed long-term relationship, and I wouldn't settle for someone who wasn't sure. **I KNEW WHAT I WANTED! (This really helps in life).**

In order to make this a possibility I had to tell him.

Hesitation was present because of my sensitive past. I wrote a letter because I usually express myself more clearly on paper. Then I called my friend Mark.

He said, "Dude, why don't you just call him?"

It's always best to keep it simple. He was right. The letter was a bit dramatic.

It was uncomfortable for me, but I called him. He picked up.

Surprisingly, there was no hesitation or stuttering on my part. I knew exactly what I wanted and wasn't afraid to ask for it. My tone was light and matter of fact.

He said, "Hm. We have really good chemistry but overall I don't know...I feel like our dynamic is meant to be more friends."

I said, "Are you sure?"

He said, [pause] "...Yeah."

I hung up the phone.

On my bed I sat quietly for a few seconds.

HOLY SHIT. I wasn't upset.

This was the day I've been waiting for, and it seemed to happen all of the sudden.

All the personal growth I had done paid off. I felt a little bummed because it would have been nice if he were on the same page, but my world didn't come crashing down like it did with past "endings." I felt empowered being self-expressive and doing what I needed to do to create what I wanted.

throws confetti in the air

HOW TO BUILD RESILIENCE

There are things we are naturally good at and some things we have to learn by "building that muscle."

I'm wired to be a highly-sensitive person with things like personal rejection or feeling like I'm not important.

If I never did personal growth in the area of rejection, communication, and breaking down my stories, I wouldn't be married to the awesome person I am married to now.

If you avoid anything that makes you uncomfortable, you won't build resilience and life will be a struggle.

My mother is a fantastic example of this. She was forced to leave her home in Cambodia during the 1970's as a refugee. Her challenging life experiences shaped her into who she is: a strong, grounded woman. She has a high tolerance for pain and I have rarely seen her freak out.

Growing up she would often say to me in Cantonese, *"Mm paa,"* which means, *"No need to be scared."*

This is why I constantly make an effort to get out of my comfort zone. To be scared and still leap. So I can grow and build that muscle.

This way adversity won't be as much of a struggle and life will feel . . . easier.

- 26 -
Be Honest With Who You Are

When I lived in NYC after college I dated a professional chef. He worked at a popular restaurant in Tribeca, and I loved going in to sit at the chef's counter to eat the food he cooked.

One time he asked if I wanted to help him with a private catering job. I did. He and his Sous Chef had an assistant chef who looked up to them a lot. She was young, sweet, and would mimic the funny things they would say. I thought it was cute, and while I was happy to help, my long-term goal wasn't to work in the catering world, supporting someone else's dream full time.

Another time I was on the phone with him while he was talking about training his staff. I was getting ready during this conversation, putting on my shoes, and admit I was not doing a good job listening. It upset him, understandably.

He was accomplished but sensitive. The kind of partner he wanted was someone whose main role was to be supportive and to look up to him. That was not me. I had my own career route I was focused on, and though now I'm much better at listening, being someone's type B support partner isn't who I am. I'm type A and do well with someone who is equal, meaning we both support each other, or I would do well with someone who is type B and plays the more supportive role to me. Me and the chef? We were too much alike.

Of course in a relationship there should be mutual support, but my point is, if I were to have stayed with him, it would not have been true to who I am. Sure there were things I liked about him, but overall I would have felt drained, doing things that didn't come naturally to me (like catering events all the time).

Deep down I would always be hoping he'd do the same for me in return, which he wouldn't because everything was mostly about him and his career.

I didn't want to become a smaller version of me. I want to be the biggest baddest version!

Being true to myself is important because I refuse to live a lie.

If I could go back and give myself one piece of advice it would be: You do you and the right people will come.

Live your truth.

Don't only do it for yourself. Do it for others. Be you. I'd hate to learn that someone was faking it with me, so I refuse to fake it for others.

How To Build Confidence

How confident are you, really? Most of us are confident in certain areas - like our careers and hobbies, but we lack confidence in other places - like intimate relationships. Sound familiar?

When you meet someone who exudes confidence, it makes an impact.

One time I was at a nightclub in Paris. My friend met up with a friend of hers who lives there.

This guy LOVED to dance. On the dance floor he punched his hairy arms into the air in the most off-beat, fantastic way. I say fantastic because he had a huge goofy smile on his face while he was doing it.

From a technical standpoint? Horrible dancer. But energetically? He was like a magnet and everyone wanted to dance with him! He was care-free, confident, and having a great time.

We should all work for that kind of confidence in our lives, right?? How many of us actually dance like no one is watching?

5 THINGS I PERSONALLY DO (OR HAVE DONE) THAT HELP ME BUILD CONFIDENCE:

1. BE ON YOUR OWN

Be single. Move away from familiarity. Take solo trips. If any of these make you uncomfortable and you refuse to do them, I think you're missing out on a huge opportunity. The message you are giving yourself is that it's scary to do it alone.

Moving away from home after college and experiencing that I could make it on my own was a mega confidence booster.

Today – eating solo, doing activities alone, and enjoying my own company is a regular confidence booster.

If you don't like hanging out with yourself, who else will?

2. TAKE A TRIP OUT OF YOUR COMFORT ZONE

The two trips I have taken that were notably out of my comfort zone were going to the Amazon rainforest in Brazil, and the Kono region of Sierra Leone. Both pushed me mentally and physically. I remember being thirsty and not having access to clean water. Bugs...huge bugs EVERYWHERE - the crunchy kind that like to nest in your hair. Ew.

I imagined getting lost and not being able to find my way home forever.

I learned that after being uncomfortable for a few days, eventually you surrender and realize everything is fine. My biggest takeaway was knowing that I don't need the things I thought I needed. I'm not going to die if I only eat stale bread everyday. I'm not going to die if I smell like cow poo and haven't showered in a week.

Soap/shampoo/dishwashing liquid – Soap is fucking soap, and I was happy to have it. Organic, cruelty-free shea butter concoctions can go suck it!

Becoming less needy = massive confidence booster. Having these experiences also makes me incredibly grateful for what I do have (like organic, cruelty-free shea butter concoctions).

3. REALIZE THAT YOUR BRAIN BELIEVES WHAT YOU TELL IT

Many of us will see a picture of ourselves and cringe, or blame ourselves for everything that goes wrong. My go-to response to myself when something didn't go as planned is, *"Great, you messed things up AGAIN!"*

First, that is not true. It is simply a habit (I made that story up when I was a kid). Second, how would I feel if someone else treated me that way? If my significant other cringed and pointed out what he thought was wrong with me? Some people allow that in their lives because they don't know how to treat themselves better. I do not, nor should you.

Anyone who's going to be in my life has to at the very least treat me with the same respect that I treat myself.

I also get in the habit of complimenting myself and say things like, *"Dang, I'm good!"* or, *"Wow, I'm proud of myself."* Your brain believes what you tell it.

4. EXERCISE

When I exercise I feel strong physically, but more so mentally. I feel great when I hike to the top of a mountain or master a new yoga pose, but the underlying thing that REALLY boosts confidence is the ability to motivate myself to get off my butt and do something good for my body.

You only get one body in this lifetime. Take care of it.

5. PUT SOME EFFORT INTO HOW YOU DRESS AND WEAR WHAT MAKES YOU HAPPY

Especially in a rut, clothing is an easy way to change things up.

My mom gave me this piece of advice when she was pregnant with my sister. She said she felt down and realized all she could do was try her best. Dressing up made her feel better.

I think making an effort to look and feel good is a sign of self-respect, and a by-product is that other people can appreciate it too!

If I'm having a hard day, I like to put on a little make-up, curl my hair, and wear heels. It's fun and indeed makes me feel a little better. And whatever I wear, I wear it for me, not because I think other people will like it.

Wear what makes you feel good and happy.

- 28 -
Show Yourself Some Love

List all the things you love about yourself. Go beyond your career and achievements. What emotional and physical qualities do you love about yourself?

If you are having a hard time listing things, you could have more self-love work to do. I've heard women say about other women, "God, she's in love with herself," like it's a bad thing. We need to flip our thinking about that!

Good for her! Maybe she shows it in a way you wouldn't. You do you and let her do her. The most important thing is to acknowledge that you feel good about yourself and what you have to offer.

Some things I love about myself:

- I'm smart
- I'm open to trying new things
- I do the work to be the best version of myself
- I love my body and all that it does for me
- I love that I'm sensitive
- I love that I'm thoughtful
- I love that I'm reasonable
- I love that I'm funny (most of the time)
- I love that I'm independent and capable
- I love that I'm fair

- I love that I have integrity

ACTION STEP:

Your turn. What do you love about yourself?

ARE YOU TELLING YOURSELF THE TRUTH?

Lies We Tell Ourselves

These are things I've heard women say to me, and things I have also experienced.

"I FEEL LIKE THERE ARE NO GOOD GUYS LEFT."

I hear it from single women all the time, and I used to believe the same.

What you believe and what you tell yourself will be true for you. Not only will you find every reason to support why you're right, it may even cause you to not "see" your person when they are right in front of you.

For a while I believed there were no good men available who were honest and devoted. That was based on previous experience and a narrative from my childhood.

It's not true. I looked around at my guy friends and my friends' husbands. They're fantastic men with integrity! The ones I knew happened to be taken, or if they were single, I simply wasn't attracted to them.

There are a lot of great guys at the activities you choose to do. There are a lot of great guys at the overpriced grocery store you go to. There are a lot of great guys at the conferences you attend. Abundance, not scarcity! It's all about your mindset.

Put yourself out there. Get to know people. Even if it's not romantic, connecting with solid, fun people feels good, doesn't it?

The person you'll match up with may be more rare, but that's what makes them special.

CASE IN POINT: YOU CAN MOVE ALL THE WAY TO THE PERUVIAN JUNGLE AND STILL FIND YOUR SOULMATE

One time I took a trip to Peru with friends who grew up there.

On our road trip from Lima to Machu Picchu, through the mountains and jungles of Peru, they wanted to visit a friend who had moved to the boonies.

We pulled into a long dirt driveway where there was a cute two-story blue home.

The friend was tall, handsome, wore reading glasses, and had long brown hair in a ponytail (this was before the "man-bun" was a thing). His gorgeous wife offered us tea as I played with their 8 year old daughter and her golden retriever puppy in a back-lit field. Like, the type of picture-perfect stuff you see in movies. The dog's name was Peaches for crying out loud.

Upon chatting over tea, I learned that he had met his wife 10 years ago in the middle of the f-ing jungle.

Yes. After college he was called to move off the beaten path because he loved being in nature.

One day she was visiting the jungle with her family. They connected, fell in love, and she eventually moved and joined him. They had a daughter and built the two-story blue home together.

While we were having tea I looked at the knick knacks on one of their desks. There was a framed photo of the two of them laughing in a hammock before their daughter was born. They were one of those stupidly good looking boho couples who look like they belong in an Anthropologie catalog. They had the same smile and energy. You could feel they were soulmates.

So if you are feeling cynical, remember that this dude met his soulmate in the middle of the Amazon jungle where he maybe comes across 100 people per year.

You can change your perception. It may take a while to re-wire your brain, but be diligent with affirmations. Do things to support the belief that your soulmate is out there and coming for you.

He (or she) is on the way.

If you expect it that person will show up.

"WE HAD SEX. I DON'T KNOW - IT WAS ONLY OK."

If you have a guy who is good at first-time sex, you have a guy who is good at first-time sex. He's probably had first-time good sex with a lot of people. Nothing wrong with that, but if you're looking to build a relationship, the first-time sex won't be an indicator of whether he will make a good partner.

Don't be so quick to judge! Maybe the person was nervous. If you liked other things about them and want to explore more, give it a chance. A slow burn can create fantastic, intimate relationships.

Side note: Pheromones are a real thing - you cannot force scientific attraction. I had a boyfriend during my 20's who was super compatible emotionally but our pheromones were not compatible. I didn't like his smell, even when he was freshly showered. If pheromones are important to you and you are pheromonally repulsed by someone, that is mother nature. I'm not a scientist, but I'm pretty sure that is impossible to change.

If it is not a pheromonal thing, but more so rhythm, timing, and technique, consider giving it a chance. Maybe they can improve (and if they never do and it just doesn't work for you, that's ok!). But remember - just because someone knows what you like off the bat is not an indicator of a good partner.

One time a girlfriend told me to not go on another date with a guy because we had already gone on three dates and he still didn't kiss me. He was so nervous - I could feel it every time he dropped me off after our dates. She was repulsed when I told her. By this time I had built more empathy and remembered that there have been times I have been really nervous, so I gave him a chance. In the long run it didn't work out between us, but I still enjoyed dating him for the time we did.

"THE GUY HAS TO BE SMARTER AND MORE CAPABLE THAN ME, OTHERWISE I GET TURNED OFF."

We live in a time when women are extremely capable. It is unfair to write someone off because they don't know how to do something better than you.

Now, I completely understand the feeling. One time I asked my husband to change the lightbulb on one of the recessed lighting fixtures in our bedroom. Recessed lighting is different from changing a regular lightbulb where you usually just unscrew it. He had never changed a recessed light before, and as I watched him poke at it, I started to get impatient.

I tried to explain how to do it properly, but he either didn't understand or ignored me.

He grabbed the tube that the lightbulb was sitting in and before I could yell, "Nooooooo!" he pulled the entire thing straight down with such force that it caused the lightbulb to shatter over us.

After hiding my face from flying shards of glass like I was in a 5th grade earthquake drill, I looked up in disbelief and said,

"WHY WOULD YOU DO THAT?!"

It took a lot for me to not make the situation worse. We cleaned everything up and eventually the lightbulb got replaced.

I went into my office the next day and told my officemate Amit the story. Amit is a very fair and evolved guy.

"It's funny how the male and female brain work COMPLETELY differently," I said.

He said, "Yeah. Women tend to have fine motor skills while men have gross motor skills."

Meaning men typically see the overall bigger picture/end result. Women are looking at the details and process.

I said, "How on earth would someone think that forcefully pulling the entire thing down would be a good idea? Wouldn't you shake or twist it a little first?"

He said, "Hm, what would I have done?" He leaned back in his chair with his hands behind his head and looked up as he was thinking... "I think I would have pulled it straight down as well."

Like my husband, my officemate, and many male brains, in a scenario like that all they see is (caveman voice) "Tube! Out! Must pull down!"

And there is nothing wrong with it. It's just different from how female brains tend to operate.

Being good at something is not the tell-all of a good partner.

What *is* important: Are they a good person? Do they put forth effort? Are they there for you when times get tough? Because I guarantee you just because someone is talented doesn't mean that they'll show up for you.

Honor your preferences, but know the difference between your negotiables and non-negotiables.

My favorite things about my husband are his patience, his kindness, and his generosity.

I also love his height, his salt-and-pepper hair, his work ethic, his love for community, his responsible spending, his fashion sense (90% of the time), his family, his taste in food, how funny he is when he drinks, and his openness for travel and trying new things.

It's okay to me that Pete had never changed a recessed light before.

- 30 -
Passion and Plateaus

"Most of us are conditioned to desire the act of falling in love instead of the act of keeping the love." ~ *Vienna Pharaon, LMFT*

Passion is an easy way to start something. Anyone can do it!

"Holy crap I met this awesome guy – we have amazing chemistry, he's cute, I can be quirky around him, and he makes me laugh like no one else can."

Then enter a challenging moment in the relationship. You realize that while you have great chemistry, he's cute, you can be quirky around him, and he makes you laugh... you've never talked about your core values and discover they don't match. You believe in integrity while he thinks it's okay to lie. You believe in putting each other first while he runs whenever he feels uncomfortable. The same problems show up repeatedly and never get fully resolved. You go back to passion + sweet moments for a while, but ultimately it feels like running a marathon.

Not sustainable.

There needs to be a strong foundation – something to hold you steady no matter what.

What's going to keep things going when passion isn't there to rely on?

When I first met Pete, besides looking googly-eyed at a handsome man, I observed his core values. I looked at whether what he said and what he did matched. I looked at how he showed up when I wasn't feeling my best. I looked at his relationship with money. I looked at his relationship to health and his body. I looked at how he interacts with not only me, but with his friends, family, and strangers. Pete later told me that he "evaluated" me in the same way.

If one of us felt unsure about something, we talked about it and made sure it was resolved so we felt confident that this was going to work long-term.

Together we built a foundation, and we are continuing to build it.

One time someone told me getting married is committing to getting to know someone throughout a lifetime. I like that.

ACTION STEP:

What have you been choosing in
previous partners that you would like
to change or be more open to?

Name Your Non-Negotiables

Decide which are preferences and which are non-negotiables.

My Non-Negotiables:

- Integrity
- Interested in me romantically and only me
- I feel safe
- I feel self expressed
- Emotional intelligence
- Empathetic
- Respects himself
- Respects others
- Loves to travel
- We have great chemistry
- Hardworking

My Negotiable Preferences:

- Similar taste in food
- No kids from previous relationships
- Good aesthetic taste

I changed and fine-tuned my list as I dated and learned more about myself. I also made a non-negotiable DOES NOT list.

After dating certain people I learned things I did not want, like I did NOT want the 40-year-old party boy. I wanted someone fun but their party days of popping molly on the weekends were out of their system.

A couple of my other do not's:

- Does not smoke
- Does not have unresolved issues with exes

Remember that your non-negotiables should be core value things and not trivial things that can close you off to a great match.

Is there such a thing as having standards that are too high? Not if you're happy! Some people might tell you your expectations are too high because they don't believe it's possible, which brings me to another point – I only take advice from people who are where I want to be.

The people who told me my standards were too high were not in the kind of relationships I wanted to be in. If they were, I would happily listen to their feedback.

- 32 -
The Panther And The Tortoise

When I first met my husband and got to know his married friends, I noticed a lot of them were in a similar relationship dynamic to us. Their wives were powerhouse women: Directors, lawyers, on-air hosts, and professional dancers traveling the globe for work.

His guy friends were grounded, type B, and had stable careers.

I'm not saying to go out and find a grounded, type B guy with a stable career. Everyone is different, and I don't know what you personally want or need! I'm mentioning this because this dynamic, in a practical sense, works well for a lot of people in our friend circle.

Pete hangs out with his guy friends because they have similar interests and values, and they chose their wives because they are compatible and complementary to their personality traits.

We joke that our marriages are like "The Panther and the Tortoise."

I love Pete's qualities of being grounded, patient, and stable. He's my rock! The flip side to that is he can move at a glacial pace compared to how I like to operate. It makes me want to roundhouse kick him in the ass, literally. Maybe it will make him move faster?

They say the thing you love most about your partner is also going to be the thing that drives you crazy. When it comes down to it, I would choose a patient partner over an impatient one, any day.

I have a sense of urgency in my work life and when I'm hanging with my hustler friends. With them I can talk shop, be efficient, post to social media, and do that part of me. With Pete, it's different. We balance each other.

- 33 -
Adjust Your Expectations

You should not lower your expectations, but do you need to adjust them?

Expecting one person to be your EVERYTHING is not fair.

As mentioned, the thing that drives me the most insane with Pete is how slooooow he can be. He's a content guy who doesn't feel the need to have a sense of urgency.

It's unfair of me to want a partner who is patient, gentle, and supportive when I need it, while also being extremely driven, quick, and efficient when I need it. That is two different people!

Everyone has a desire to feel safe. Everyone also has a desire for adventure and unpredictability. You can get a balance of both, but it may not align all the time.

It's not realistic to expect to get every single one of your needs met from one person unless they are a robot.

Psychotherapist Esther Perel says that villages and communities are how humans were made to survive. People in a village have different skill sets and contribute in different ways. Expecting one person to fulfill everything a village provides is impossible. The same goes for romantic relationships.

- 34 -
Finding A Well-Rounded Happiness

Friendships, particularly with my female friends, are fulfilling. There is an understanding they can give me that a male partner never could.

Like one time my girlfriend sent me a photo of a loaf of white bread. She said she told her husband she was hungry and asked if he could bring something back.

All she said was *"WHYYYYY?"*

Why out of all things would he bring a plain white loaf of bread with nothing to go with it? Peanut butter? Baloney? Anything?!

All I responded was, "Some things your girlfriends will always do better..."

For reference, I would have gotten her something heavier if she was "in a mood," like a slice of veggie pizza or old-fashioned donut, and something healthier if I knew she was on a health kick, like a well-massaged kale salad with almonds. In return she would know exactly what to get me if I told her I was hungry.

Besides my marriage, having a healthy community is important to me. It makes life more fulfilling. Plus you have more people holding you accountable, which minimizes the chances of you going off the deep end.

I want to be the person who makes an effort to maintain a social circle and other areas of my life that I associate with "me." My husband feels the same and has his career, guy time, and hobbies. Neither of us can be everything for the other person.

THERE ARE A LOT OF JOYS IN LIFE OUTSIDE OF A ROMANTIC RELATIONSHIP

You might intellectually know there are other things important in life besides a romantic relationship, but reaching the point where you feel it is the goal.

Once you find yourself in that long-term relationship, you will truly feel that being in it is not as dramatic as you made it out to be.

Do you know that feeling when you reach a work goal you've always wanted? In your head you dream of the day you're on the Ellen show, coming out as she announces you, doing a dance, hugging her, and sitting down for an interview. You put it on your vision board.

When the day actually happens, usually it's not this OMG feeling. It's more like, "Oh. Huh. I did it."

It's surprisingly calm and not as big of a deal as you made it out to be in your head. There is the romantic anticipation of it, and then there's the reality part of it.

Your health is important. Self love is important. Your friends and family are important. Your hobbies are important.

Life can be fulfilling without a romantic partner, I promise you.

ACTION STEP:

What else is important to you besides a
romantic relationship? What will you be
thinking about when you are on your deathbed?

- 35 -
Increase Your Happiness

I keep a notebook on my nightstand. It's been a game-changer for me in terms of recognizing happiness. Every night before I fall asleep I write down at least five things that were good about my day.

SOME EXAMPLES FROM YESTERDAY:

- Wearing my new super soft new robe for the first time.

- How the guy at the juice place knows that I don't like my smoothies too sweet, so upon ordering he said, "no agave, right?"

- My best friend from Canada calling and making me laugh for 15 minutes.

- Wrapping a birthday present and having the perfect amount of wrapping paper left to just cover the box.

- Putting all my laundry away and having no stray clothes laying around (finally).

I love this ritual because it trains your brain to look for the positive instead of the negative. Some days have more obvious things than others, but there is something to be grateful for every single day.

Try it for at least a week (or more!), and pay attention to how your happiness level shifts.

KEEP IT REAL. KEEP IT HONEST.

Master The Art Of Communication

My friend Mark called and said, "I arrive on Wednesday at 6:30pm."

Whenever he comes to town he stays at my place, but this time I was feeling overwhelmed and didn't feel like having anyone over. His assumption made me agitated.

I often go to Mark for advice because he is a great communicator and he is also a relationship coach. It's interesting typing that out - *great communicator + relationship coach* - because it shows how crucial good communication is to have a good relationship!

Whenever I complain, the first thing he says is, "Have you told the person?" which is usually followed with a "No."

Then he says in a *duh* tone, "Why don't you just tell them? How are they supposed to know what you need if you don't say anything?"

COMMUNICATION IS LOVE

Sometimes I have a hard time communicating what I need out of fear. Fear I'll hurt someone's feelings, fear of criticism, or fear of rejection.

My concern this time was I didn't want Mark to think I was a crappy friend, but I got over it, called him, and said, "Hey. I'm in a place where I need space right now. Can you stay somewhere else when you come?"

Immediately I felt relieved. THAT'S ALL I HAD TO DO.

He said, "Sure. Thanks for telling me. Is everything ok?"

I said, "Yeah. I'm just feeling particular about having my own space."

And once again, as he always says (but this time referring to himself), "Thanks for telling me, otherwise I wouldn't know what you need, and we'd have one of those shitty relationships where we can't properly communicate!"

And there it was.

Being a shitty friend would have been to NOT say anything. If I didn't say anything, I would have resented the poor guy when he came. Getting mad at someone and blaming them for your unhappiness is unfair when you don't do your job of telling them how you're feeling.

I had a conversation with someone about communicating the other day and she said, "But whenever I try to tell someone something like that, they get mad and defensive..."

My thoughts about that:

- I've learned how you say something, the words you choose, make all the difference. Take responsibility for how you feel instead of blaming the other person. When Mark told me he was coming, my first thought was – Ugh, I'm busy and I don't like when people assume they can stay at my place. All victim and blame. So I took a deep breath and accepted responsibility. "Hey, I feel like I need space right now." What a world of difference it makes in how someone receives it!

- The truth is you can never control what anyone's reaction will be. For me, I surround myself with people who are conscious, empathetic, and emotionally intelligent enough to not take things personally, and if they do, they communicate it well. They'll say something along the lines of, "I'm so bummed you can't make it to my birthday party!" versus "I can't believe you're not going to come. That's messed up."

Self-expression is liberating and a huge confidence booster.

Being honest, taking responsibility, and having the courage to communicate what you need – It's the only kind of relationship I choose to have in my life, and I'm thankful for the people who give it to me in return.

- 37 -
When Your Needs Just Don't Align

When my 14 year-old dog passed away, I was a wreck.

My friends and family showed up and were super supportive. Even my exes who I hadn't spoken to in years shot me texts when they heard from mutual friends or through social media. But the guy I was dating at the time? Crickets.

He distanced himself and sent a couple awkward texts. It felt crappy because I really wanted support from him, but he didn't know how to show up the way I needed. My pain made him uncomfortable. This was a major red flag for me.

I knew it was for the better. I wanted a self-aware guy who wasn't afraid of intimacy. I scared him off early with the death of my dog (can I laugh about it now?). I wanted someone I could fully be myself around, good emotions and bad.

That being said, there is a balance, and timing could be a thing.

Sometimes there is such a thing as putting too much pressure on someone you barely know, and the range is different for everyone. I've done it and have had it done to me. Your long-time friends and family may not see it as pressure, and it may be more appropriate to go to them versus someone you don't know as well.

But again, you do you and the right people will come.

HOW OPEN IS TOO OPEN?

This is the flip side.

One time I had someone rent out my spare room for a few weeks while she was in town doing a therapy program. She told me she was doing a program to heal, and she was in the heat of it.

She was in a vulnerable state, and I was extremely uncomfortable by how much she so deeply wanted to connect because I was focusing on my own life at that time.

To me the room was a rental transaction, but she was looking for way more. A couple weeks in she told me she was unhappy staying at my place because she didn't feel welcome. She literally said there were too many pillows on my couch so she felt like she couldn't sit there. I told her that she can move the throw pillows like everyone else if she wanted to sit on the couch. After that she went out and bought me a book from her therapy program and wrote me a three-page letter thanking me for the talk, and telling me she analyzed my behavior and thinks I have blocks to love.

I have no problem doing this kind of exchange with my friends or life partner, but for someone I barely knew, I was repulsed. For me it was way too much analyzing, eagerness, and desperation.

But maybe others would be okay with it and would want to connect back. Again, the range and timing is different for everyone. The person who is right for you will love you with open arms, however you may be feeling.

All I know is that I always want to feel like I can express myself fully around my partner.

WHAT TO DO IF YOU ARE GOING THROUGH SOMETHING EMOTIONAL WHEN YOU'RE WITH SOMEONE NEW

Ahh, the art of communicating. You absolutely should be vulnerable and share whatever you are going through with someone, but the trick is to not push it on them. People pick up when you push your emotions onto them, and last time I checked, no one likes that.

- 38 -
Set Your Intention While Dating

It's great that you want to find your forever person! However, if that is your main goal when you go on dates it will exude energy that can be straight up terrifying to whoever is sitting across from you.

Have you ever had it done to you? To me it felt like the person was not present, and it never felt good.

Instead of putting on that pressure, go on dates with the intention of having fun and connecting with people. That is a fantastic starting point which can lead to something more serious down the road.

Life is meant to be enjoyed, just like weddings are for celebrating.

If it starts to get stressful, ask yourself: *Why* am I doing this?

To feel good. To feel good. To feel good.

Don't aim to get it right. Aim to feel good.

- 39 -
Seek Feedback From Those You Trust

It can be tough to get feedback. Sometimes people care about you and don't want to see you get hurt, so they'll say things that aren't supportive.

I have been guilty of doing this to friends. One time my friend wanted to date this guy who notoriously cheated on every girl he dated in the past (I knew some of his exes). I thought, "Why the F would you want to date him?"

I wasn't very supportive because I knew what the outcome would be.

A few months in things didn't work out (thank god).

She said, "You tried to tell me and I didn't listen."

Here's the thing - It's not my job to save her. I'm much better at communication now, so if it happened again, I would inform her in a more practical way: by asking her questions and giving her facts if she asked instead of bombarding her with what I think would be best.

Because the truth is, I don't know what's best for her! She's on her own journey which is different from mine. Not to mention, I've dated ding dongs before. Maybe she needed to experience dating someone crappy at that point in time so she could get clear on what was good for her.

Ask your friends and family who are good communicators and who you TRUST, for feedback.

I asked my friend Jake for feedback once when I was dating. Jake is a lawyer. He is level-headed, fair, and I admire his marriage.

He said, "Maybe you come off too intense when you first start dating someone."

As soon as he said that I nodded, "You're right."

I could feel the energy I was exuding on dates. Especially if I liked the person, I was secretly nervous and hoped they liked me too - to a fault. People can feel the pressure even if you don't say anything about it. I've had it done to me before and didn't like how it felt on the receiving end.

This was something I wanted to be more aware of. I knew I wanted to be fully ME on dates, but my goal was to have more fun instead of hoping for an outcome, which... can come off as intense.

I wanted dating to feel light and easy, and that was up to me.

My friends and I still ask each other this question from time to time: "Is there anything I can work on to be better in this area of my life?"

If you're offended at what your trusted friends say, that is an unhealed part of you. Or, maybe you need to get new friends who are better communicators.

Anyway, ask your friends. Or a good therapist

40

Where Are All The Good Men?

SOME PRACTICAL TIPS

DO THINGS THAT INTEREST YOU

Dance class, book clubs, kayaking, restaurants you like... do things you are truly into. The least you'll get is meeting people who have similar interests, which is already pretty darn fulfilling.

BE STRATEGIC ABOUT WHERE YOU GO TO POTENTIALLY MEET PEOPLE

I used to go to happy hour with another single girlfriend in certain neighborhoods in LA. We chose places with a more refined atmosphere because we liked the food, the cocktails, and the crowd. We strategically chose those spots over a $1 beer happy hour dive bar. Fantastic people are everywhere and liking $1 beer isn't a bad thing, but we wanted to increase our chances of meeting people with similar taste.

BE OPEN TO ONLINE DATING

Some people hate online dating. I say only go on it if it feels good. Overall it can be a great opportunity and tool to meet someone. I can't tell you how many weddings I have photographed where the couples met online. Smart, successful, wealthy, sexy couples! But if you are in a depressed, hopeless phase and feeling burned out, maybe take a break from it.

GO SOMEWHERE THERE ARE PEOPLE

If you put yourself around more people, the higher the chance you have of meeting new people, period. I met my husband standing on a corner waiting for an Uber.

TRUST FRIENDS TO MAKE INTRODUCTIONS

This is one of the best ways to meet someone and minimizes the chances of them being a looney sociopath.

When I met Pete my client who introduced us (and now our mutual friend) told me, "Pete is the salt of the earth, I'm not joking."

He was right.

You really never know where you'll meet someone. The most important thing is to stay open, be around people, and have fun.

YOU DON'T NEED TO MEET YOUR SOULMATE TO HAVE A FANTASTIC DATE

I was in India at a wedding, getting ready to call it a night. On my way out I walked past a group of guys and one of them said, "Hey, you're the photographer from LA, right? The groom told me about you...I'm applying to go to film school in NYC or LA."

We talked for two minutes and connected on WhatsApp. While in India, all my time had been consumed with the wedding so I hadn't gotten a chance to see anything. A couple days later it worked out that my afternoon was free. I received a message from him:

"Have you seen Mehrangarh Fort?"

Me: "No."

He said I should definitely see the Fort.

"Pick you up at your hotel at 3:00?"

"Ok..."

He showed up wearing Marc Jacobs sunglasses and a blazer.

"I'm going to change, I came straight from work."

When we arrived at the Fort, he handed me a ticket, headphones, and sent me on my way in.

"I'll see you back out here in an hour."

I looked at him confused. "You aren't going to come in?"

"I've seen it a million times. I'll give you space to explore it on your own, and I know you'll want to take photos. Meet you back here in an hour or so!"

The Fort was amazing. I listened to the audio tour and spoke to some locals. They asked to take a picture with me as they giggled and threw up peace signs.

I walked by a sign that said, "Palm reader." One of the things I really wanted to do while in India was get a psychic reading. Excited, I stepped into the tiny office. The man was in his 60's and looked like a professor. Mustache + glasses + maroon sweater vest. For 600 rupees (10 dollars), he took one glance at my palm and told me EVERYTHING about my personality. He knew when I had met the loves in my life. He knew I changed careers at 26. He knew I had one sister and that my mom tied her tubes after having me. He knew things about me I've never told anyone.

Just as he was finishing, the office phone rang. He said a few things in Hindi and then nodded his head twice. He handed me the phone.

"It's for you."

Perplexed is an understatement. Who the HECK would be calling me in a tiny psychic shop in India? I slowly put the rotary phone to my ear like I was in the Matrix...

"Hello?"

"Hey, get down right now! We're going ziplining and the last group is leaving."

"Uh...ok. How did you know I was in here?"

"Don't worry about it... We gotta go!"

I handed the phone back to the palm reader.

He hung it up, smiled, and said, "What did I tell you? You have a lot of admirers."

I gave a hesitant smile, handed him 600 rupees, and walked toward the exit. There stood my date.

"Seriously, how did you know I was in there?"

He smiled and said, "I just knew."

In my heeled boots I clumsily ran through the cobblestone streets. He laughed and asked what size shoe I was. I said 39.

We arrived at the ziplining office. He threw me a pair of size 39 sneakers and his buddy strapped me into a harness while handing me a clipboard saying, "Sign here." We ran a bit more (much easier in sneakers) and before I knew it I was strapped to a zipline cruising around town like Zorro.

"What did I tell you – it's amazing at sunset, huh?" he said.

I looked out at the blue city with the sun setting behind it. On our way out I played with a stray dog. She looked healthy and rabies-free.

My date looked at me. "Want to go shopping?"

I wanted to squeal but instead said, "...Sure!"

He took me to a hidden wholesale supplier. The shop was in the old part of town where the streets are narrow and chaotic. He laughed as he watched me dodge tok-toks and cows like we were in a video game. I ended up buying a hand-sewn rug from one of the shops.

After shopping we went to a swanky hotel rooftop for dinner overlooking the city. We drank wine and chomped on skewers. I looked out at the view.

"What are all the houses covered in Christmas lights?" I asked.

"It means someone in the family is getting married."

"Wow, a lot of people are getting married..."

It was time to call it a night.

On the way back to drop me off he said, "We didn't have dessert. Do you want some?"

I said, "Sure."

He pulled over and went up to a food cart swarming with locals.

"Here."

He handed me a condensed milk pistachio popsicle through the car window.

"It's street food, but GOOD street food."

He watched me take a bite and ran back to the stand. He came back to throw a foil plate and napkins on my lap. I finished the entire thing as we pulled up to the hotel.

"Thanks for showing me around, that was super fun. Let me know if you end up coming to NY or LA for film school."

He smiled. "I will."

There was no kiss but a nice hug.

That was the end of my awesome date in India. The details of what happened aren't important. It wasn't the best date ever because of the specific things we did or because he was my soulmate. Like with anything else in life, it had little to do with the external factors, and EVERYTHING to do with being open-minded and saying YES.

Magic happens when you say YES. Stay open to possibility.

41

Three Reasons It's Easier To Live An Authentic Life

1. IT'S FUN BEING ABLE TO BE YOU

I didn't feel comfortable being me for a good part of my adolescence, and also during a long-term relationship in my mid-twenties. I felt like I was walking on eggshells. Too often, something I did would garner criticism, disapproval, or some kind of problem. I hated that feeling, so that's why as an adult I only hang out with people who are supportive and 100% okay with me being me. If they feel uncomfortable with something I'm doing, they will talk to me about it instead of attacking me. I like that. I choose that.

Also, it's exhausting having to be "on," feeling like you can't be yourself.

2. YOU WILL ATTRACT PEOPLE WHO HAVE THE SAME VALUES AND NATURALLY WANT TO BE AROUND YOU

It takes a lot of courage to be real because it means you won't be liked by everyone. The good news is – those who love you, REALLY love you. When I started to get the hang of showing up authentically as me on dates, I made a conscious effort NOT to do anything that I normally wouldn't do down the road so they knew what they were signing up for.

Like when Billy Crystal says in the movie When Harry Met Sally, *"You take someone to the airport, it's clearly the beginning of the relationship. That's why I have never taken anyone to the airport at the beginning of a relationship. Because eventually things move on and you don't take someone to the airport and I never wanted anyone to say to me, 'How come you never take me to the airport anymore?'"*

Don't go out of your way with grand gestures in the beginning if that's not who you really are.

3. PEOPLE ARE DRAWN TO AUTHENTICITY

People find it endearing when they can tell you're comfortable sharing yourself no matter what kind of place you're in. That means showing up not only when you're in a confident, good place, but also when you're feeling vulnerable and low. People would rather hear, "Hey, I feel like crap right now," than see you with a fake smile on your face, telling people everything is perfect all the time.

Who can connect to that? Well, maybe someone who has intimacy issues and wants a robot partner. "No fake surface-level relationship wanted here," I told myself. I want to dive deep.

- 42 -

HOW TO BE YOUR BEST SELF:
The Difference Between Wanting To Do A Good Job And Trying Too Hard

There's a clear difference between wanting to do a good job and trying too hard.

When someone wants to do a good job, it's for themselves. They have self-love, and it makes them feel good. The feeling is exciting and energizing.

When someone is trying too hard, it's for other people. Their actions are hoping to gain love or approval from someone else. The feeling is desperation and exhaustion.

I used to get dressed up for dates entirely for the other person. It makes me cringe now that I think about it. It wasn't until I started to not give a fuck whether they liked my outfit (me) or not, and wore what I wanted to (for ME), that I gained confidence and felt good dating. Shortly after I made this change, I met my future husband. Coincidence?

Signs pointed to this truth long before it clicked in my brain. I remember certain instances where I forgot to change what I was wearing and felt embarrassed. To be specific, one time a guy and I were going to yoga class. He came to pick me up, and I realized I didn't change out of my house knitted booties that had pom poms on them.

This happened multiple times with different articles of clothing and different people, and kid you not, every single time, the guy always said, "You look so cute!" I thought, "I do?"

They didn't always comment on the times I really tried to look cute or sexy because I'm sure they felt...I was trying too hard. Completely different energy.

The best advice I can ever give someone who wants to find a long term partner is to be you. That sounds cliché, but it's the truth.

If you show up as you from the beginning, as in the *weird-asshole-you* that your closest friends and family see, you will set yourself up for success. You'll attract a relationship that's easy and comfortable because that person loves you 100% for being you. Don't do anything differently in the beginning unless you want to change for yourself to become a better person. If someone can get scared off, it's better to scare them off early and save time. Make room for the person who will love you for you.

I've also had it done to me – like once I dated a guy who would acknowledge if I didn't laugh at his joke. If you think your own joke is funny, why care if anyone else thinks it's funny too? One of the most endearing things is when someone belly laughs at their own joke. I instantly smile and gravitate towards them, whether the joke was actually funny or not.

In terms of my work, I always want to do a good job not so much for the client, but for myself. I feel good when I work hard and am happy with what I produce. It energizes me.

I've coached some photographers who get shattered when a client doesn't respond to their photo delivery. They are looking for validation that the client likes their photos. I typically don't wait for a response because no matter what the client says, I think my work is good and I'm excited when I send them the link to view their pictures!

Feel good about who you are so you don't have to rely on outside validation. Coming from a place of desperation is exhausting and not attractive.

Some Final Advice On Dating

There's a lot of grey area, but here is some very general advice. It's up to you to use your judgment regarding what you think would be best for yourself. And remember, finding clarity on what is best for you begins with self-awareness and personal growth. Don't forget to get to know yourself first!

1. ONLY TAKE ADVICE FROM PEOPLE WHO ARE WHERE YOU WANT TO BE

If you want relationship advice, talk to someone who is in the kind of relationship you want to be in.

2. MAKE A LIST OF YOUR NON-NEGOTIABLE TRAITS IN A PARTNER

This will save you a TON of time when dating. For example my core value is integrity. If a person shows me they don't have it, I'm out, no matter how funny, charming, or handsome they are.

3. FOCUS INWARD

While in the dating scene and experiencing break-ups/ghosting/ weird people, look at what you are learning about yourself instead of focusing on the other person.

4. CHOOSE SOMEONE YOU CAN GENUINELY BE FRIENDS WITH

If you are looking for a long-term partner, the person you want to choose is one who fulfills your emotional needs. Don't forget about them! With friendship also comes respect, which is a healthy foundation.

5. SIMILAR BELIEFS AND VALUES SHOULD BE THE PRIORITY

Lifestyle and all that other stuff is secondary. Lifestyle is workable and can fall into place if your beliefs and values are in line. If you only connect on the lifestyle and superficial stuff, it is difficult and can be impossible to work "backwards" to get your values in line.

6. A PERSON'S CHARACTER TRUMPS THEIR PERSONALITY

If you tend to go after the funny charming talented guy, make sure they have good character too. How does he feel about lying? How does he respond when he sees you upset?

7. BE YOURSELF AND COMMUNICATE WHAT YOU NEED

If someone can be scared off, it saves you time to scare them off early rather than waste your time dating them, only to have them scared off months or even years later.

- 44 -

How Do You Know You've Found "The One"?

They say "You know when you know," which isn't the clearest advice. When people used to tell me that I always wondered what "that" feeling was.

Both my husband and I did a ton of introspection on ourselves before meeting each other. We agree that instead of focusing on the other person and their qualities, it's really more important to know yourself.

YOU know when you feel at ease. YOU know when you feel inspired. YOU know when you feel good.

Know what you want, but more importantly, know what you need.

WHEN YOU KNOW, YOU KNOW

I met my friend's new boyfriend. She asked what I thought.

Me: "I like him because I like who you are when you're with him."

Her: "Really? I feel like I'm just being me."

Me: "Exactly."

A great relationship is when you love who YOU are in that relationship.

If you'd like more inspiration on life lessons and other fun things, visit my blog at www.christinechang.com.

Made in the USA
Middletown, DE
29 August 2020